DUNCAN'S PUB WALKS

Lancaster to The Lakes

by

Duncan Turner

For Alan

May your feet always be dry
and your drinks always be wet!
And thankyou for your
knowledge.

Cheers
Duncan.

Carnegie Publishing Ltd

© Duncan Turner, 2002

Published by Carnegie Publishing Ltd
Carnegie House,
Chatsworth Road
Lancaster
LA1 4SL
Tel: +44(0)1524-840111
Fax: +44(0)1524-840222
email: carnegie@provider.co.uk
publishing and book sales: www.carnegiepub.co.uk
book production: www.wooof.net

First edition, 2002

British Library Cataloguing-in-Publication data
A catalogue record for this book is available from the British Library

ISBN 1-85936-083-1

Typeset by Carnegie Publishing
Printed by The Cromwell Press, Wiltshire

Contents

The distances are as accurate as I can make them. The times are those I took on the day I walked the route, and so are just a rough guide.

The entire proceeds of this book will be given to two children's charities. Derian House is a hospice in Lancashire providing care for terminally-ill children and, like all children's hospices, operates on very little government funding. It's an expensive place to run and I hope that this book will pay for at least six hours of its operational costs, or even longer.

The other half is going to Medicine and Chernobyl UK (Ribble Valley Branch) a charity with which I am involved. Children from Belarus are brought to Britain to get away from the endemic low-level radiation which pollutes the country following the Chernobyl disaster. One month's respite during puberty will provide the children with all they need to recuperate their immune system and give them strength in their adult years to live a reasonably healthy life. It is hoped that the proceeds will be sufficient to fly two children to Britain and home again.

Derian House, Registered Charity Number 1005165
Medicine and Chernobyl, UK, Registered Charity Number 1039688

Key (and guide) to all maps

walking route		church or religious building	
canals and rivers		mud/salt marsh	
small rivers and streams		farm or work building	
roads		wind farm	
motorway		forest/copse/woodland detail	
railways		golf course	
crags or mountains		caravan park	
bridges		compass direction	
large bridge/railway bridge/ aqueduct		public house to take lunch	
water feature			
special point of interest			
water/sewage works		height of land	
start point		rock outcroppings/quarry	
direction arrow for locations outside map boundaries		beacon	
building or public house			
parking		tower	

342m   height of land

Introduction

Covering the north of Lancashire, from a line running just south of Glasson on the Lune estuary, all these walks are to a pub and back again. The pubs are usually just over half way round the route and where a lunchtime snack or meal can be taken. Lancashire's boundaries were changed in 1974 and I have interpreted the boundaries very loosely. None of the walks is in Furness and one or two barely set foot in Lancashire, but start and finish not too far north of the Cumbria/Lancashire boundary. One or two stray into North Yorkshire but are mainly in Lancashire. I'm sure you are not at all bothered by this; hopefully your main aim is to enjoy a good walk and a pub lunch!

The return journeys are usually shorter than the outward journeys which, I believe, is a good idea, especially if you've succumbed to an extra drink and/or rather more food than you intended! Most walks involve the use of a car to get you to and from your starting place, although public transport will give you access to most of the routes. Because of changing timetables and the other vagaries of buses and trains I have not included specific travel information, although I have provided 'phone numbers.

It is a good idea to have the correct *Explorer* or *Outdoor Leisure* map when following the walks. Although with a bit of skill the *Landranger* maps *97: Kendal and Morecambe* and *102: Preston, Blackpool* will suffice, the scale of these sometimes means the detail is a little obscure. The best maps to follow the walks are *Outdoor Leisure* maps *21: Forest of Bowland, 7: The English Lakes (SE), Explorer 2: Yorkshire Dales, Southern and Western Dales,* or *Explorer 296: Lancaster, Morecambe and Fleetwood.* The problem with these is that they are big and unwieldy and a stiff wind could theoretically lift the user off the ground! Personally, I find them a bit of a nightmare to use, even indoors, and it is obvious that the person (or, more likely, the committee!) who designed them never had cause to use them out in the fresh air. Of course, they could be used as an emergency tent if you had them laminated! If my itineraries are as well written as I hope they are, then you shouldn't need to refer to a map much at all, as long as you've managed to find the starting point.

None of the walks is very rigorous, although I do realise this statement could be contentious. They vary in length between about 5 and 12 miles and avoid very long uphill climbs. You will, of course, ascend gradients on some of the walks but none of the paths is steep for more than a few yards. They can also all be walked in under five hours, not including the lunch break.

It is advisable to wear good boots, together with a good pair of socks, since nothing else protects your feet so well. As good as some walking shoes are, they can be useless in mud or rough ground and do not stop your feet from slipping forwards when going downhill, as boots do. This slipping forward causes blisters on your toes, so shoes are totally unsuitable in my opinion unless walking along a very flat route without mud. If you do wear stout shoes, trainers or wellies don't blame me if you get sore or wet feet, or if you lose your grip on the ground. You really can't beat a pair of boots with a good thick sole and if you're going to walk regularly it is a good investment to get a pair. If you wear proper socks you may not need to wear two pairs, but I know some people's feet are more tender than others so a light pair under the thicker outer pair may help.

As well as good footwear it is always important to take good clothing, including a waterproof. You may set off in fair weather but it can quickly change, especially in hilly areas, and it is so miserable to be out in the rain and soaked to the skin. I know jeans are popular leisure wear but they're totally useless when wet and take ages to dry out; meanwhile you're getting chilled. Any make of lightweight windproof trousers is much better. Also, walking sticks aren't just for the old and infirm. If you've ever walked in Austria or Switzerland you'll be aware that they're for everybody – old and young alike. Not only do they help you to keep your balance on rough ground, but they can also be useful for knocking weeds aside and as a last resort may come in handy in the unlikely event of being attacked by an animal – up its nose is the best place I'm told! Oh, and it is always worth having a drink, something to nibble and a few first aid requisites with you, including a survival bag or similar. None of these takes up much room in your back pack, nor are they expensive and you never do know when you'll need them. Also your friends will be ever so impressed when you 'pull things out of the bag'!

The countryside is mainly a place of peace and solitude, just occasionally shattered by the noise of farm machinery or barking dogs, but it is also a place where danger lurks just as readily as in the urban environment. Always be aware that uneven paths, foot-bridges and muddy slopes can be lethal. Potholes can be masked by long grass and abandoned ironmongery can do you real damage if not noticed. Stiles which often pass over lethal barbed-wire, have loose footplates, can be slippery in wet weather or go over really high walls, can also cause damage to your person. The drivers of fast-moving and large vehicles on country roads do not always expect to come across people on foot and particular care should always be taken, especially when approaching blind bends where, if you are walking to face it, the oncoming traffic will bear to the right. Always walk in single file on roads where there is no footpath.

Most farm dogs bark at you but that's what they're trained to do and they're usually tied up anyway. However, it has been known for cows, as well as bulls, to charge people, especially when they have young calves with them. Just like us they protect their young should they feel they're under threat. I'm sure you already know all this but it doesn't do any harm to be reminded. So don't sneak up and startle them but steer well clear and perhaps make a noise long before you approach them.

These walks are all designed for a day out, say leaving home at 9.30am and arriving back home at about 4.30pm, with time for various breaks and at least an hour at lunch time. If you find the walks tiring you may not be fit enough. If you're at all uncertain perhaps the best approach is to try one of the shorter walks to test your 'walkability'. The walks have all been undertaken by people between the ages of 53 and 68 years, so any reasonably fit person of that age group, or younger or older for that matter, should be capable of doing them. Many will be suitable for young children over the age of eight years, though I'm sure younger children could also enjoy them.

The distances quoted are reasonably accurate, having been measured carefully on the map, checked with a pedometer during the walks and then checked again. The walking times are only a guide, since it depends on how fast you walk, or whether or not you linger to admire the view or watch wildlife. Younger people will possibly cover the ground quicker than the 'ageing juveniles' who tested them out. Walks in flat country, those mainly to the west of the M6 and in river valleys, will inevitably be covered quicker than those in the hillier parts. The average walking time works out at about 2.4 miles per hour, so if you're going uphill it will be less than this and if you're travelling on the flat, especially along a road, you will be quicker and probably be approaching 3 miles per hour. The weather also makes a difference to the time taken; sunny days and days with good visibility will tend to make the walks longer in time. On miserable days the tendency will be to step out and get to the pub and back to the car as fast as possible, instead of stopping to enjoy the views, watch wildlife or spot interesting flora.

Whatever speed you walk or however long it takes I can guarantee that you will enjoy the glorious splendour of our north Lancashire countryside as you walk the pathways and bridleways, towpaths and lanes, fields and moorlands. Our countryside is precious; do look after it. Don't leave gates open, don't frighten sheep – or farmers, who are mostly friendly and pleased to see and help you. It is important to remember that the paths across farmland are Public Rights of Way but you shouldn't stray off them. If you keep to the paths, no one should bother you. If you do come across an irate farmer it is probably best to apologise and seek his help in getting on the right route. Arguing seems out of place in the countryside and it is amazing how often the farmers are flattered when you bow to their superior knowledge. Do take away your litter, or anyone else's for that matter. It is your countryside but you don't own it, though I do hope you cherish it.

Just to remind you of the Rights of Way Act 1990, these are the salient points:

1. If a path runs across a field the farmer is allowed to plough it to cultivate it but must make it good again within 14 days.

2. If the path is around the edge of a field its surface must not be ploughed or disturbed.

3. The path must be at least 1 metre wide.

4. Farmers must make the line of the path apparent so that walkers can see where it goes.

It is obvious that some farmers don't or won't obey the law but I still maintain that any unpleasantness on your part will not solve any problems. Farmers have a tough life and can often be under great stress for a whole range of reasons. If you have any problems and have the time and inclination a letter to the County Council's Footpaths Officer may solve them and at the same time assist him in his task of maintaining the paths.

When we visited the pubs mentioned in the book we thought they were worth visiting and we enjoyed our simple bar lunch and drink. Just like the countryside you walk in, pub landlords change and some are better than others. I can't guarantee the pub will meet your expectations and just to be certain that it is open it is worth phoning the pub before you set off. If you'd rather take a picnic, you can of course start these walks anywhere. They're all circular and as long as you go in the same direction you shouldn't have too much trouble following the route. On the other hand you may fancy a challenge and walk the routes 'widdershins' – in the opposite direction, and why not; you'll just have to read the instructions upside down or walk backwards! Starting the walks at the pub and returning there for a drink at the end is always an option but I suggest you mention it to the landlord before you set off.

Some of the walks may seem similar to others at a brief glimpse but they all either end up at a different pub or follow a different route. They really are all different – even the two walks which circumnavigate Barbon Low Fell. One follows a clockwise route, the other an anti-clockwise route and the difference is amazing.

Finally, the disclaimer. The information and directions are given in good faith that they will be accurate forever. Realistically this will not be the case since we live in an ever-changing world. The countryside is forever changing and routes may be changed, though this means they should be clearly marked. Stiles may disappear and so may gates, hedges and other landmarks as detailed. Indeed, since I started recording these walks in 1995 I have repeated them all and on every occasion some detail has altered. It is not usually a major change, perhaps just an improved path with new stiles, but nonetheless a variation on my original written route. This will inevitably be the case when you come to follow the instructions. Also, do not assume the information regarding the geography, topology and history is totally accurate.

It has been written by using what I have read in a wide variety of books, learned from others or by just using my own limited knowledge in interpreting what I have seen.

When you have completed all the walks you will know the way to walk from Cockerham, in the very south of the area, all the way to Burton-in-Kendal, and by going on a road for only a few hundred yards. Or, if you wish to walk west to east, you will know how to get from Hest Bank to High Bentham in a similar fashion, although you will have to cover longer stretches of this walk on the road. The simple fact is that all the walks connect up, with the exception of the stretch between Aldingham and the Lune Viaduct, but all you have to do in order to complete the link is to walk north along the towpath through Lancaster, possibly stopping off at *The Water Witch* for refreshment.

I should like to mention the good companions with whom I have walked these routes and whose company I have enjoyed through many years, during many a mile and over many a pint. First of all my wife, Carole, my constant companion in life as well as a good companion on very many walks. An especial mention must be made of my old friend Bill Pickering with whom I first remember walking in 1955 and who has walked nearly as many of these walks as my wife. His knowledge of birds and other country matters has also been most welcome, not forgetting to mention his scrutiny of the script to ensure that you don't turn left when you should have turned right! I've learned a lot at his side and I shall be forever grateful. I must not forget my other companions with whom I have walked for years: Peter, Bill the Wiganer, Ian, John, Bob and Bert. Having spent my entire working life as a bookseller I am aware that you would not be reading this book without the input of many people. First of all Anna Goddard and her colleagues at Carnegie Publishing who took the risk of putting this into print. Secondly, the booksellers who also took the risk in purchasing it and putting it on their shelves. Thirdly, the people who purchased it, whether or not it was yourself or someone else. Thanks to you all.

Happy walking, I hope you enjoy them as much as I have done and do take care of yourself and your walking companions.

Duncan Turner 2002

Walk 1

Aldcliffe to Conder Green

Explorer map 648:   *Lancaster, Morecambe*
                           & Fleetwood
Distance: 7.75 miles   Walking time: 2 hrs 55 mins
Start at canal bank, Aldcliffe, grid ref: SD469604
Lunch at *The Stork*, 01524 751234

A RELATIVELY short, flat walk starting with a long stretch along the Lancaster Canal towpath and, on the return from Conder Green, another long flat stretch along the old railway line by the estuary of the Lune. Not being elevated there are no views of note, unless you get a clear view of the Lake District on the return route. There is also a chance of seeing a lot of birds both along the canal and the Lune. Mainly good paths but the stretch across the fields from the canal to Conder Green may be slutchy in places.

🚶 Leave your car on Aldcliffe Road by the canal side, where there is a convenient lay-by, and head off south along the Lancaster Canal towpath in the direction of Galgate. After walking along the towpath for about 1200 yards, or 15 minutes or so, you enter into what is known as Deep Cutting, which is self-explanatory.

❶ *In fact the first bridge you come to (No. 94) with an enormously high arch is named Deep Cutting Bridge. The cutting is just about a mile long and ends at bridge No. 92, but even after that the sides remain heavily wooded, which maintains, to a degree, the dank and rather forbidding atmosphere, especially during the dark days of winter.*

🚶 After stepping out for about 3 miles (roughly one hour) you will be arriving at the outskirts of Galgate where you will see bungalows on the opposite bank. Go over the stile on your right and bear diagonally right across the field towards the trees and then alongside the fence and through a gate. Now look out for a stile on your left which leads you into the woods. Follow the path up through the trees, over the stile and then up and across a field,

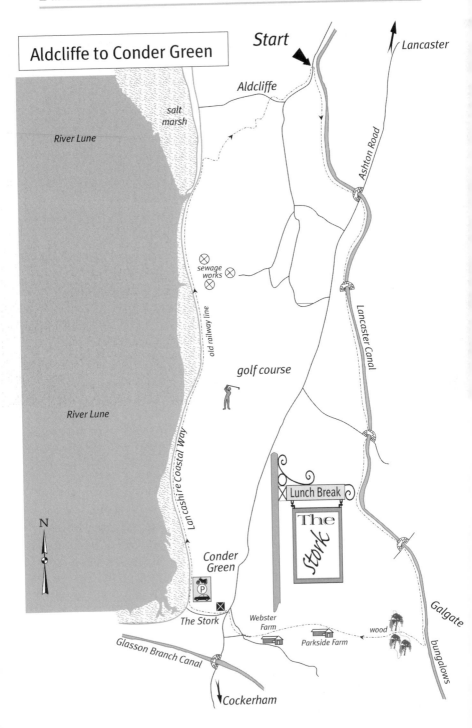

Aldcliffe to Conder Green

Start

Lancaster

Aldcliffe

salt marsh

River Lune

Ashton Road

sewage works

old railway line

golf course

Lancaster Canal

River Lune

N

Lunch Break

The Stork

Conder Green

The Stork

Webster Farm

Parkside Farm

wood

Galgate

bungalows

Glasson Branch Canal

Cockerham

Deep Cutting bridge (No. 94), Lancaster Canal.

bearing slightly to your left. Go over a stile and down to the next stile by a gate and then follow the fence round to your right. Go under the overhead wires and at the next gate go to the other side of the fence, turn left and follow that down to Parkside Farm. Here you go through the farmyard and carry straight on to Webster's Farm, where you bear right round the farm buildings then go over a footbridge to your right over which you turn left to follow the fence down towards a stile and on to the road. Turn right and follow the road to *The Stork Hotel*, which is the white building you can see about 400 yards away, for lunch. (4.45 miles; 1 hr 35 mins)

On leaving *The Stork* turn right and follow the road towards Glasson and the River Lune and then bear right to follow the old railway track north along the Lancashire Coastal Way in the direction of Lancaster.

❶ *You are now walking along an old railway track which linked Glasson to Lancaster. It was opened in 1887. There was a station for Conder Green at the car park and picnic site where you are now standing and the fare into Lancaster was about 3 old pence (1½p). The first passenger train along the line apparently departed Lancaster at 9.15am and arrived in Glasson at 9.25am and well over 100 years later there is not a chance that anyone could repeat the journey from the middle of Lancaster to Glasson in so short a time, no matter what form of transport they took, save a helicopter, but it is doubtful if one could land in the middle of Lancaster. Perhaps we're not as advanced as we sometimes think we are! Passenger trains stopped running in 1930. Goods trains ran daily until 1947 and the line was finally closed in 1964. Over to your left you will have a good view of the Lune estuary which is a Site of Special Scientific Interest (SSSI), since it supports what is probably the largest population of wintering and passage population wading birds in the country. If you're there at the right time it will amuse you to spot as many varieties as you can as you walk along. Grey heron, shelduck, oystercatcher and redshank will almost certainly be around at any time of the year. In the winter you may see cormorants, wigeon and snipe, and passing through in winter you may glimpse dunlins, curlew, sandpipers, green sandpipers and common sandpipers. These are just some of them; there are of course many others.*

⊛ After about 2 miles, or 50 minutes if you haven't dawdled, go down and over a stile on your right; this is just after the path veers away from the river. You can just about see Aldcliffe diagonally up and to your right. Follow the fence up the field, over the stile and turn left, over another stile where you carry on upwards bearing right a little. Over another stile and then along the passage to Aldcliffe.

❶ *Aldcliffe is an ancient village but it doesn't appear to be so old and it is difficult to believe it was there at the time the* Domesday Book *was written. It is probably named after a Norseman named Alda.*

⊛ At the lane turn right and at the T junction turn left and walk down the road, taking care to avoid fast-moving cars, and back to the canal side where you left your car. (3.3 miles; 1 hr 20 mins)

Walk 2

Aughton to Arkholme

Outdoor Leisure maps 41: Forest of Bowland & Ribblesdale
7: The Lake District SE Area
Distance: 10 miles   Walking time: 4 hrs 10 mins
Start at centre of Aughton, grid ref. SD 550672
Lunch at *The Bay Horse*, 015242 21425

THIS WALK has two stiff ascents, one on grass, the other on the road. Neither are very long; on the way out it is 75 metres (250 ft) and the last lap home is on the road 50 metres (160 ft). You also walk a considerable part of the route alongside the Lune, so this is flat. A good stretch is over fields so expect 'bog' after wet weather.

There aren't many places to park a car in Aughton so it may be that you start quite a way from the centre of the hamlet. However, from the crossroads walk down the lane which is marked as a cul-de-sac and which leads you down to the bottom of the Lune valley.

Like many habitations along the Lune valley, Aughton, pronounced Afton, has been here a long time. It is a 'ton' or homestead of Anglian origin and its earliest recorded name is Acheton. Also, like many other villages and hamlets along this stretch of the Lune, basket-making from the willows which grow along the banks of the river was a traditional occupation. Cut in early spring the willows were heated in a boiler to make them supple. Known locally as 'wand weavers', the craft thrived until the mid-nineteeenth century when it gradually died out. In 1781 two brothers who were both weavers bought a new, much bigger cauldron for heating the wands and it is reputed that someone said it would make a great pudding boiler. The next year a pudding was boiled for two days, and thereafter every 21 years, a pudding festival was held. Each year the pudding became bigger and bigger. After the demise of willow weaving this custom died out but was revived in 1971 and another festival was held in 1992. If you're a pudding fan you can always look forward to 2013 when no doubt another great pudding will be boiled.

11

Aughton to
Arkholme

Lunch Break

Bay
Horse

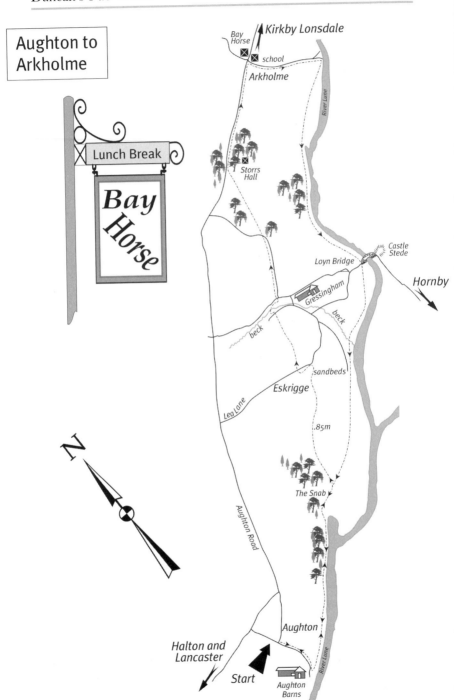

Kirkby Lonsdale

Bay
Horse

school

Arkholme

Storrs
Hall

River Lane

Castle
Stede

Loyn Bridge

Hornby

Gressingham

beck

beck

sandbeds

Eskrigge

Lea Lane

.85m

N

The Snab

Aughton Road

Aughton

Halton and
Lancaster

Start

Aughton
Barns

River Lune

(🏃) As you arrive down by the two cottages at Aughton Barns take the stile on your left over a ditch and into a field. You are now on the path of the Lune Valley Ramble which you will follow for the next mile, or about 25 minutes. Head across the field and you will see a gate and to the left of this is a stile, so go over and on to the next stile and soon you approach the bank of the river. Almost straight away you have to go up the slope on your right and then over another stile into Great Close Wood and below on your left will be an islet which is now overgrown. The path through the wood has been managed and there are wooden-fronted steps and the path has a retaining plank in parts to stop you sliding down towards the river. This is a slightly tricky section where you need to take care where you put your feet because exposed tree roots are an ever-present threat to your stability; you also have to keep an eye out for twigs and brambles which may catch your face. You emerge out of the wood and onto an open platform of grass near a bend in the river and from here you will have a good view of Hornby Castle and, on a good day, Ingleborough in the far distance. You're soon back into trees and then the path goes behind a house onto a track. This is The Snab and you turn right on the track and pass a small pond on your right. Soon there is a footpath off to your right but ignore this and carry on up the slope and just where the track bends left go through the gate on your right, just before the barn. There is a stile in the fence ahead which you go over before heading to the top of the field where the row of trees is to be seen on the skyline. The next gate is to the right of the trees in the corner. Keep to the left of this field with the hedge on your left hand side and head for the crown of the hill up ahead.

(ℹ️) *From this vantage point you will have splendid views south over the Lune Valley and Caton Moor, with its eerie, electricity-generating wind-mills on your right, and on a clear day you will also have a first-class view to the left, or north, towards the Lakeland fells and further to your left, or north westward, Morecambe Bay. You will also have climbed up 75 metres (250 feet) from The Snab.*

(🏃) Carry on with the hedge down on your left and through a gate in a fence. Turn sharp left and through another gate where you turn sharp right to follow the hedge and the ditch on your right. Soon you come to a signpost, a concessionary path goes to your left, but we go over the stile and straight on across the field. As you pass under the overhead power lines you will spot another stile in the hedge by the corner. Go over this and follow the green lane ahead between two hedges. The one on the left is mainly holly so be careful of overhanging branches. The path soon ends near to Belle View farm and you carry on until you come to a lane. Turn left here and just past the house you take the footpath to the right, the one to the left is where you would have emerged if you had taken the concessionary path earlier. Go up the track and over the stile beside the wall of the house on your right. The path follows the hedge on your left and at the top over a stile in the corner. As you go down the next field you will see a gate below you and to the left of this is a stile leading into another field. Here take the footpath to the left, following the fence, and to another gate with a stile next to it and you are now on a track which leads you out onto the road in Gressingham, famous for its duckling which you will find in all the best restaurants round these parts. Turn left and at the barn marked Box Tree Farm turn right and down to the steps which lead you over two foot-bridges crossing the stream. Take care whilst going down the steps, I know someone who slipped badly and gave himself quite a shock here – me! Over the bridges go up to the road and cross over to go up the road next to the Old School. At the next junction turn left uphill and follow this for about 600 yards. Whilst doing so I suggest you keep to the right and in single file (as you should whilst walking along any road) since this can be quite busy being the shortest route from the Halton to Kirkby Lonsdale road down to Loyn bridge. As the road bends left and up there is a gate on your right. Go through into the field and bear slightly left. In the distance you will see a tall tree standing up amidst lots more trees. This is a good marker for the next 600 yards, so head straight towards it. Soon there is a stile and carry on following the faint path in the field in the same direction. There is another stile and now you have a clearer view of Storrs Hall to the right of the tall tree. The next stile is at the left-hand edge of the beech hedge, so go through into a passage and then through a gate onto the road. From here it is about 15 minutes (1200 yards) into Arkholme. Keep to the right again and in single file walk downhill into the village. As you get to the Methodist Chapel, cross over since there is a nasty bend ahead, and you are soon on a pavement which

Loyn bridge. The motte and bailey, Castle Stede, is behind the trees.

takes you to the crossroads and *The Bay Horse* where you will be able to get refreshments. (4.8 miles; 2 hrs 5 mins)

Ⓧ Having been suitably refreshed turn left out of the pub and down the road beside the school, across the main road. This road is a cul-de-sac and leads to the church and to the river side.

ⓘ *As you walk along this lane you may wish to note the names of some of the houses and conjecture why they have been so named, Caulking House, Phoenix House, Reading Room Cottage being three which spring to mind.*

Ⓧ As you approach the church take the right-hand fork pointing to the river and on your left is the church on a little knoll.

ⓘ *Arkholme was established by the Norse and is recorded as Ergune, the place (or shieling) at the hill pastures, in the* Domesday *survey. The land is the site of a motte and bailey. At one time it was a chapel to the church in Melling across the river where the inhabitants had to go for weddings and funerals. To do this they had to go by ferry and the old ferryman's cottage is further down the lane on your right. It became a parish church in its own right soon after a wedding party perished whilst crossing over the river.*

Ⓧ Down by the river you once more find yourself on the Lune Valley Ramble and you will be following the path all the way back to

15

Aughton. This first stretch is well marked and there are lots of little yellow arrows pointing the way. Certainly if you keep the river on your left you can't go wrong. Just as you can see Loyn bridge having walked about a mile there is a post with an arrow pointing to the right, but you go over the stile on the left and soon you're at the bridge.

🛈 *Across the bridge is a slope and at the top is another motte and bailey known in days of old as Castle Stede. It is not very obvious when the leaves are green but during the winter months you can quite easily discern the earthworks through the trees. There is evidence of a Saxon or Danish fort here before the Norman motte and bailey.*

🚶 Cross over the road and go over the opposite wall by using the steps in the wall and follow the path to the river bank and to the other side of this very big field. A footbridge leads you into the woods and very much like the paths through the woods you trod earlier it varies in quality, so watch how you go. Incidentally, the

The 'slab stones' at Aughton Bottoms.

footbridge is marked as a 'ford' on some older maps. As you emerge from the woods you will see a signpost over on your right ahead. Go to that and carry on keeping to the path indicated and it again follows the river. Just over on your right you will soon see where the River Wenning rushes into the Lune. Pass through a gate beside a fisherman's hut and bear right towards the trees. Soon you will be near to the pond you saw earlier and this is The Snab again. Go through the gate and onto the track. It should be quite easy from now on since you simply retrace your steps to Aughton, but first of all remember to turn left just past the cottage.

❶ *As you walk through the last field approaching Aughton Barns you may wish to ponder upon the flat slab stones sticking up in the field. They look a little like headstones in a graveyard, yet they don't have inscriptions; they are obviously not natural and have been placed there by someone. I have been told that they are the 'slab wall' remnants of a Norman boundary but could be older.*

As you walked down the lane from the hamlet to the barns you may have noticed how steep the hill was. If you didn't you'll surely notice on the return but just console yourself that it is a good way to finish in style – with a bit of effort!

❶ *A good way to take your mind off the problem is to cast your eye to the hedgerows and the banks upon which they grow. In summer it is a good idea to count and identify the flowers; in winter you can try to spot plants that wouldn't be so obvious in summer. Before you know it you'll be at the top of the hill!*

⊛ Eventually the hill becomes easier and soon you'll be at the crossroads and back at the car. (5.2 miles; 2 hrs 5 mins)

Walk 3

Barbondale to Casterton

Explorer map 2:	Yorkshire Dales – Southern and Western Areas

Distance: 9.8 miles   Walking time: 4 hrs 25 mins
Start at Blindbeck Bridge, grid ref: SD656828
Lunch at *The Pheasant*, 015242 71230

THIS IS THE SAME ROUTE as Casterton Fell Yeat to Barbon but is walked in the opposite direction; anti-clockwise or 'widdershins'. It is still a delightful walk and it is still not in Lancashire. I also believe you will enjoy it as much as the clockwise route but, as recommended, try to do it at a different time of the year. Also some of the cross field stretches can be slutchy.

During our walk, late in September, we found 15 varieties of fungi; some poisonous, some edible. We found them out on the fellside and in Barbon Woods. At the right time of the year you may find yourself sufficient for a pleasant meal – if you know what to look for! If you don't, beware, since picking and eating mushrooms if you don't know what you are doing is a bit like playing Russian roulette.

Park your car on a convenient verge near the bridge and set off by taking the path up Aygill to Bull Pot Farm. The path is on the right before the bridge as you come up from Barbon and is marked by a finger post. The route goes up the gill below Lower Barbon Fell, up on your right, and after a gate you walk down a green lane between stone walls down to Bull Pot Farm. Turn right up the road for about ½ mile then take the path through the gate on your right marked by another finger post. Down to your left you will see Gale Garth farm. Follow this good path gradually up and round Brownthwaite Pike, the fell up on your right, and through three gates before coming to a gate in a wall on your left. This leads down another green lane to the road you left earlier. Turn right downhill and after about 800 yards, just after going through

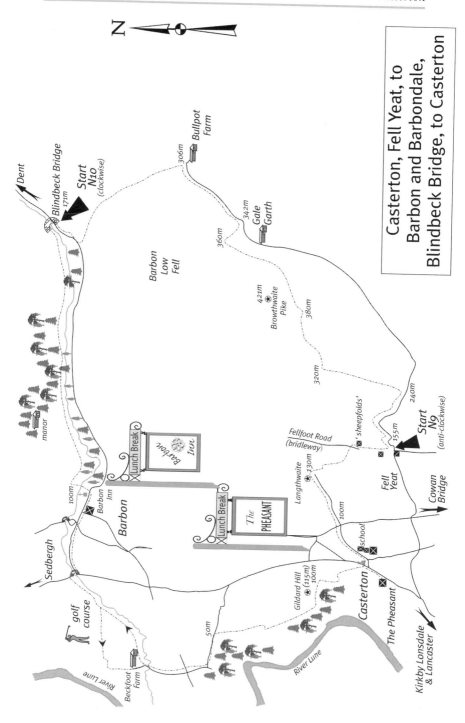

Casterton, Fell Yeat, to Barbon and Barbondale, Blindbeck Bridge, to Casterton

*One of Andy Goldsworthy's 'sheepfolds' near to the road
up to Bullpot Farm.*

a series of bends in the road, take the green lane known as Fell
Foot Road on your right. The finger post calls it Bents Lane.

ⓘ *As you walk along look out for the strange sheepfolds with boulders
inside them in the fields adjoining the lane. These were constructed in
1996 by Andy Goldsworthy, whose skill and fame as a constructive
artist is spreading throughout the world. What you will make of these
structures depends on your outlook on art. He has constructed 100 of
them in Cumbria, with the aid of a County Council grant. Not only
does he construct in stone – he has constructed a 10-foot high acorn
shape near his home – but also uses many natural, short-lived materials
including trees, flowers, leaves and even wool. Using this latter medium
he lined the top of a stone wall which he had seen earlier covered in
snow! Holland, Nova Scotia, Japan and the US mid-west are just
some of the venues for his creations.*

ⓧ Opposite the third structure, which is on your right, take the path
through the gate on your left and head diagonally right across
the field to the gap in the wall. At the other side turn left and
walk along the wall until you emerge through a gate onto a lane
at Langthwaite. Turn left and follow the lane down to the crossroads, across and under the bridge, past the school and into
Casterton. Go past the church on your right and out onto the
road where you turn left and soon you are at *The Pheasant Inn* for
lunch. (4.8 miles; 2 hrs 10 mins)

❶ *The name of the village suggests it was at one time a camp or castle; it is very near to a Roman road, but no evidence exists to prove it. Casterton School was founded in 1823 as the Clergy Daughters' School, with benefits particularly for the daughters of clergy with the smallest incomes. The girls there now come from a much wider background. If you were fascinated by the creations of Andy Goldsmith you may find an in-depth description of his work inside the bar of The Pheasant.*

🚶 Leaving the pub turn left and retrace your steps but keep to the left-hand side of the road. Just as you reach a 'School' road sign take the footpath on your left and go through a narrow gap in the wall pointing to Lowfield lane. At the bottom carry straight on, up the incline and steps between the buildings and through the gate at the top with a small stone building next to it. Follow the wall on your right-hand side, with the school playing fields on the other side, past the old barn and down to the gate. Turn right and up the field with the boundary on your right, through two sets of gates and out into another field. Turn left and bear right slightly up the incline of Gildard Hill, making a line halfway between the copse at the top of the hill and the wood down on your left.

A distant view of Gildard Hill, with Casterton School playing fields in the foreground.

ⓘ *Why such a small hill should be given a name puzzles me. I can't find out why it is so named; perhaps it was named after someone. On the other hand, it could have been named centuries ago and entitled by early map-makers with a name which sounded correct. For instance 'cilearda' would mean 'the retreat of a man called Earda'.*

☭ Then make for the left-hand side of the big tree and straight on for the stile down in the corner. Go over the stile and straight on down across the field heading for the step stile over the wall ahead and then straight on again across the next field making for the bushy tree at the corner of the wall. Go to the left with the wall on your right. Go through the gate on your right and then follow the fence on your left, past the blasted oak, and to Lowfields Lane. Turn left and follow the lane under the old railway bridge to Low Beckfoot Farm, carrying on to Beckfoot Farm. Here follow the path to the right-hand side of the house and over a stile and follow the path with Barbon Beck down on your right. You make for another stile across the field then onto the golf course, keeping to the indicated path and keeping watch for low-flying white balls! You have right of way along the public footpath but sensibly there is no need to fall out with those who 'spoil a good walk'. At an opening in the wall, just past a tee, bear right and back to the banks of the beck and follow the path round the fringe of the golf course to the road at Hodge Bridge. Turn right and then left over the bridge and follow the road to Barbon.

ⓘ *At the time of the* Domesday *survey the manor belonged to Tosti, the Earl of Northumberland, and was known as Berebrune. The present, well looked-after and obviously much-cherished, church was built in 1815.*

☭ Go past *The Barbon Inn* and the church and take the track on your left just past one which leads up to Barbon Manor. Despite the notice advising you that you are on a private road it is a public right of way for those on foot, so go over the bridge and follow the track till it approaches the woods at the top of the hill. There, 250 yards after a sharp bend with a barrier placed to deter cars from driving over the edge, there is a signpost directing you towards the woods. Take this path to the right and through the gate to follow the path up through the very attractive private woods. Do keep to the path and you'll be all right since it is still

The River Barbon near Blindbeck Bridge.

a right of way. You eventually emerge out of the trees and soon you will come to the beck near where you parked your car earlier. Walk up to the bridge, cross over and back to your car. On the other hand if the water is low enough and you are nimble of foot you may wish to use the stones in the beck to hop over the water and back to your car. (5.0 miles; 2 hrs 15 mins)

Walk 4

Bull Beck to Claughton

Outdoor Leisure map 41:   Forest of Bowland and Ribblesdale
Distance: 6.6 miles   Walking time: 3 hrs
Start at Bull Beck Bridge Car Park, grid ref. SD 544650
Lunch at *The Fenwick Arms*, 015242 21250

A SHORT WALK perhaps best suited to winter, or if time is short. It rises from 23 metres to 258 metres near Claughton quarries but it is a steady climb through fields and on the road. On a clear day the view from here is tremendous and you can see Black Combe and Barrow in the west, and right round to Ingleton and further east, so that in a glance you can see almost half way across England. A cold clear day in winter is the best time. Good paths and a return alongside the Lune.

IMPORTANT – Before setting off on this walk read the PLEASE NOTE in the introduction to the return journey on page 27.

(🏃) Turn left, or east, from the car park on the road to Claughton (pronounced Claffton) which is in fact less than two miles along the road, although it is going to be a couple of hours before you get there. After 100 yards you take the stile on your right. Head up the field bearing right and over a stile then carry on to the top right-hand corner of this field and through a snicket onto a road and you are now in Brookhouse, part of Caton. Turn left and right at the junction, past the church and at the pub turn left and left again over the bridge.

ℹ️ *The church of St John has a Norman doorway which is intriguingly blocked up with medieval grave slabs. The church was rebuilt in 1865 with the exception of the tower. This old village has houses which were originally built in Elizabethan times but they're hard to detect. Set into the bridge as it turns up to the Littledale road is where, during the Great Plague, money was dipped in vinegar and left there in exchange for provisions.*

24

Bull Beck Bridge to Claughton

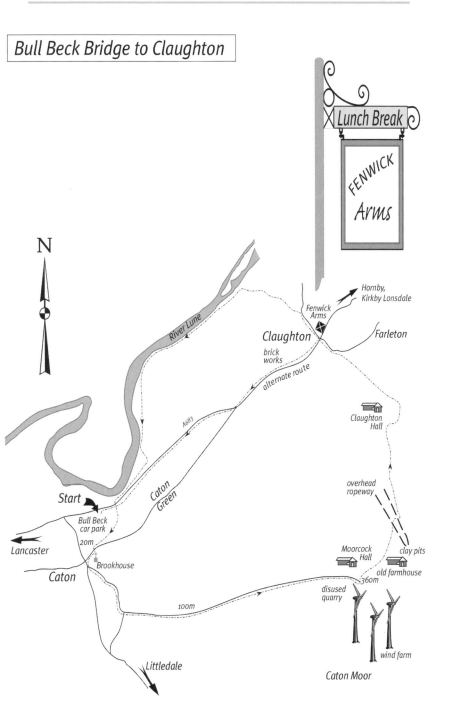

N

Lunch Break

FENWICK Arms

River Lune

Hornby, Kirkby Lonsdale

Fenwick Arms

Claughton

Farleton

brick works

alternate route

A683

Claughton Hall

overhead ropeway

Caton Green

Start

Bull Beck car park

20m

Lancaster

Brookhouse

Caton

Moorcock Hall

clay pits

old farmhouse

360m

100m

disused quarry

Littledale

wind farm

Caton Moor

🚶 Turn left over the bridge and go up the hill and turn left again at Moorside Farm following the road uphill for almost 2 miles until it turns into a track near to the 'ominous' windmills.

ⓘ *On a good day you if you look north you will have a wonderful panoramic view of the Lakeland Fells and the Pennines as far round as Whernside, and if you're really lucky you can also see Black Combe behind Barrow. So if the conditions are just right you can see almost half way across England!*

🚶 At the windmills you go over a stile and down and to your left following the path along the contour line past the disused Moorcock Hall farmhouse where you then go downhill, through a field and over a stile. Turn sharp right to the gill that leads out of the quarry and follow this down, keeping the trees on your left.

ⓘ *Here you will notice the overhead ropeway built in 1922. This was used to take clay down to Claughton Brickworks down in the valley.*

🚶 This path eventually brings you onto a track skirting round the estate of Claughton Hall and which is protected by a stout wire mesh fence. (To keep people in or out, I wonder?)

The lepers' or plague bowl set into the bridge at Brookhouse.

A close-up of the lepers' or plague bowl at Brookhouse.

🛈 *Originally the Hall was built down in the valley in the seventeenth century. There is uncertainty about the exact date or even which King was on the throne; some documents refer to James, others to Charles I, though there's no doubt it is a Stuart building. Early parts are supposed to have been built in the thirteenth century. The important detail is that about half the original was taken down and each stone moved to its present site to be rebuilt in 1935. Just one wing of the original building was left in place and that is now Claughton Hall Farm.*

🚶 Eventually you reach a lane which you follow down to the main road, turn right and have lunch at the *Fenwick Arms*. (4.2 miles; 2 hrs)

PLEASE NOTE.

Just before going to press I discovered to my dismay that the 'after lunch' route back from The Fenwick Arms, as printed below, isn't open. The problem is that a section of the path, very close to the finish, has fallen into the river and the owner of the land will not allow walkers to enter his private property. In time, and when you decide to follow this route, the path may be open but meanwhile the only alternative is to follow the road west, towards Lancaster. Regrettably, and with all due respect to the inhabitants of Claughton, this is not the most scenic of roadside routes. It is easy to check whether or not the path is open before you set off since there is a notice board by the path opposite the Bull Beck car park. As you start off you will be able to cross over the road and drop down to the old railway line and follow it east, towards Hornby, where the board is situated just where the pathway joins the pavement alongside the road.

(🏃) Leaving the pub, turn right and down the lane on your right. If it is not raining heavily and the Lune hasn't burst its banks head down the lane which you follow for about 400 yards before climbing over a stile on your left. Over the stile turn sharp right following the fence on your right, then after about 200 yards bear slightly left for the gate in the next fence and then, bearing slightly left again, cross the enormous field towards the river which you then follow left in a westerly direction, or with the flow.

(ℹ) *This stretch of river is popular with anglers as it meets EC prescribed levels of quality, except for nitrites. It is also popular with birds, probably for the same reason. Watch out for goosanders, they swim with their heads under water and the male has a black stripe down its back. There will also be oystercatchers who favour this stretch too.*

(🏃) Where it bends round to the left the path wanders away from the bank and goes over a footbridge then back, following the river for another 300 yards before turning sharp left, across a stream and then right until you come to the old railway line which you follow until you espy the car park from where you departed earlier. (2.4 miles, 1 hr)

Walk 5

Bull Beck to Halton

Outdoor Leisure map 41:   Forest of Bowland & Ribblesdale
Distance: 9.0 miles   Walking time: 3 hrs 40 mins
Start at Bull Beck car park, grid ref. SD 544650
Lunch at *The White Lion,* 01524 811210

A VERY FLAT WALK, since this follows the Lune all the way there and back, with just the exception of a short climb up through some trees on the way back. Parts of the walk can be slutchy after wet weather but on the other hand quite a lot of the route is along very good tarmacked paths. A good winter walk.

🚶 Cross over the road from the car park and down the steps to the old railway line which is now a footpath. Turn left, or west, towards Lancaster and follow the path to Crook o' Lune.

ℹ️ *The railway line was opened in 1850 by the North Western Railway Company to run from Lancaster to Wennington, where it joined the Skipton to Carnforth line. One of the interesting facts about its beginning is that the coaches and wagons originally supplied were of a different gauge to the locomotives, thereby causing considerable embarrassment to the director who ordered them! Passenger services ceased in 1965 and part of the line was kept open to serve Lancaster's coal-burning power station. The last train ran in the mid-1970s.*

🚶 Cross over the bridge above the Lune and take the path down the steps on your right. This takes you through the woods and along the river. Follow this as close to the river as you can go until such time as you have to climb up to take to the old railway line again. This is just past the water pumping station by the weir. Follow the path as far as the Lune Aqueduct and having gone under it bear left and ascend the steps to the towpath and turn left to go over the river.

ℹ️ *The aqueduct was built in 1797 to the design of John Rennie at a cost £48,321. The span of the four piers is 70 feet each and the overall*

Bull Beck Bridge to Halton

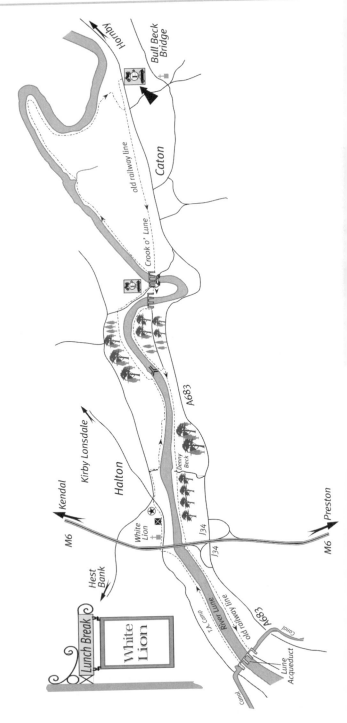

Rennie's aqueduct over the Lune.

length is 664 feet. The water in the trough is 53 feet above the surface of the river. At the time of its construction it was the longest aqueduct in the country.

🚶 Across the aqueduct immediately drop down the path on your left, through some bushes and down to the river bank and then under the aqueduct soaring overhead. The path then leads you east with the river on your right, past the TA Training Camp, and out onto the road by the motorway. Turn right under the bridge and follow the pavement into Halton where you can get lunch at *The White Lion*. You can also have a bite and a drink at *The Greyhound*, further up and to the right at the crossroads. (5 miles; 2 hrs 10 mins)

ℹ️ *Halton is an ancient village and was the administrative centre for the area during Saxon times – for some reason or other they seemed to have ignored the Roman remains at Lancaster. The church of St Wilfrid stands on a Christian site pre-dating the Conquest, though the age of the church isn't obvious following major rebuilding in 1792 and later in the nineteenth century, with the exception of the perpendicular tower. In the churchyard there is a Norse preaching cross. On one side is the Ascension of Christ and on the other is the pagan story of Sigurd and Volsung, a not uncommon occurrence showing how the early Christians kept their options open! The head of the cross was added in 1890 by enthusiastic, if not misguided, Victorians who wanted a complete cross. There is a Norman motte and bailey above the village on Castle Hill just past the crossroads on the road to Hest Bank. You can see a flagpole in its centre as you walk up the village.*

After lunch turn left out of the pub and uphill to the crossroads where you take the right fork. Then, just after *The Greyhound*, turn right towards the old bridge over the Lune. Don't cross this but turn left into Mill Lane on your left and follow the footpath sign along the lane until the last building on your right, before

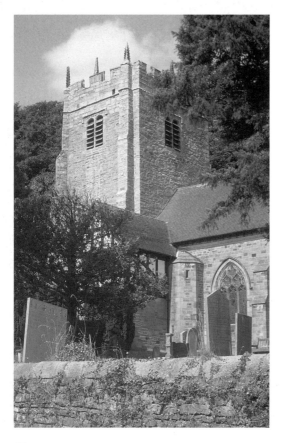

St Wilfrid's Church, Halton.

The motte and bailey at Halton.

The Lune at Halton where the ancient waterwheels were set.

the gate across the path, where you go across the forecourt of the factory and to the path along the riverside. Here you turn left and follow the path with the river down on your right.

ℹ️ *There have been mills on this site since as far back as 1251, mainly producing a variety of textiles, and there would have been a row of waterwheels alongside the river powering them. This is easy to understand when you look down at the river, especially when it is in full flood. The buildings are now used for a variety of purposes, but not textile production, as you will probably have noticed.*

🚶 When you get to the weir you climb up the steps on your left and bear right to follow the path up through the wood and out onto the road. Turn right, cross over and follow the footpath to Crook o' Lune.

ℹ️ *If you fancy a cup of tea, or some other refreshment, there's usually a mobile café here run by the estimable Woody, who was runner-up in 1998 for the best mobile café in Lancashire. By the time you read this he may have retired, but I don't doubt that someone else will have taken over the pitch. If you sit on one of the rustic tables at the lookout you can enjoy the same view as painted by the famous nineteenth-century artist, J. M. W. Turner.*

🚶 Leaving the car park go down the steps to the old railway line, cross over the bridge on your left and then go down to the left to the footpath along the river and turn right. (On the other hand, if you wish you can go straight back along the old railway line to your car.) Having walked along the river for a while you cross over Artle Beck by the stepping stones and then go past the Thirlmere aqueduct. At the next stile either carry on and follow the river all the way round the loop. This path eventually leads onto a farm track which you follow until it brings you to the old railway line again; turn left through the gate and after about 400 yards you will be back at the steps leading up to the road, over which you cross with care and you're back in the car par. (4 miles; 1 hr 30 mins)

Walk 6

Casterton, Fell Yeat Sheepfold, to Barbon

Pathfinder map 628:   *Kirkby Lonsdale & Barbon*
Distance: 9.8 miles   Walking time: 4 hrs 10 mins
Start at Sheepfold on Fell Road, grid ref. SD636794
Lunch at *The Barbon Inn*, 01524 72633

THIS WALK neither starts nor finishes in, nor strays into, Lancashire but it is only just over the border into Cumbria. A delightfully varied walk, with a fair amount of ascent. It takes in fells, country lanes and woodland pathways and stretches across fields, not to mention a golf course and a few quiet lanes. The views on a good day are memorable, both up and down the Lune valley and across to Gregareth, the highest point in today's Lancashire (not forgetting there are those who insist that Coniston Old Man is still in the County Palatine!). Mainly good underfoot, but the short field stretches can be muddy.

🏃 Start off by heading uphill (always a good way to warm up) until you come to a footpath sign on your left pointing up a lane towards the fell top. Go through a gate at the top of the lane and bear right continuing to follow the track all the way round, with Brownthwaite Pike up on your left. Don't be tempted by the left-hand fork in the track when you come across it. Eventually you come to the brow and go down, through a gate and down to come out onto Fell Road again, just above the farm at Gale Garth. Turn left on the road and follow it to Bull Pot Farm, where you turn left up the droving road to Aygill and down to Barbondale.

ℹ️ *In the autumn you will find an interesting variety of mushrooms as you walk along this track and also later on as you go down through the woods of Barbon Park.*

🏃 As you enter onto the road at Blindbeck Bridge turn right and over the bridge and up to the footbridge over Barbon Beck. On the other hand you may want to jump from stone to stone over

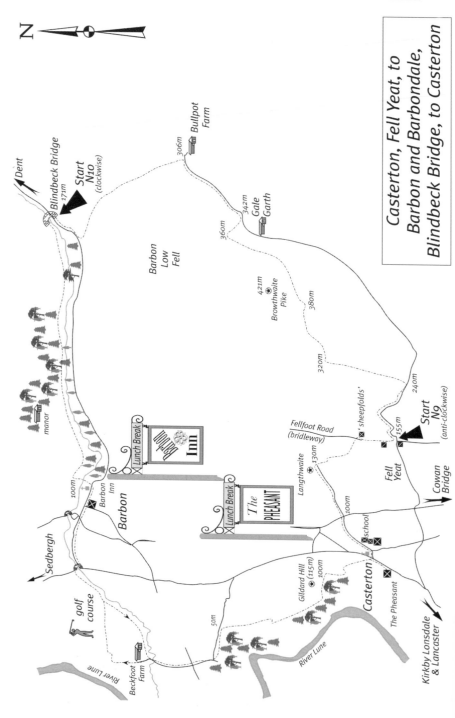

N

Casterton, Fell Yeat, to Barbon and Barbondale, Blindbeck Bridge, to Casterton

Dent

Blindbeck Bridge
171m

Start No10
(clockwise)

306m
Bullpot Farm

342m
Gale Garth

360m

Barbon Low Fell

421m
Browthwaite Pike

380m

320m

240m

155m

Start No9
(anti-clockwise)

'sheepfolds'

Fellfoot Road
(bridleway)

Fell Yeat

Cowan Bridge

Langthwaite

130m

100m

manor

Lunch Break

Inn

Barbon Inn

Barbon

100m

Sedbergh

Lunch Break

The **PHEASANT**

school

golf course

Gildard Hill
(115m)

100m

Casterton

The Pheasant

50m

Kirkby Lonsdale & Lancaster

River Lune

Beckfoot Farm

River Lune

the beck – if you slip and get wet it is your fault not mine! Whichever way you have crossed over, head back downstream, through the delightful woods of Barbon Park, which are private so do keep to the path. As you exit the woods you go through a gate and ahead onto the private road to the Manor House where you turn left, downhill and this brings you out at Barbon Church. Turn right and soon you will be at *The Barbon Inn* where you can have lunch. (5.6 miles; 2 hrs 20 mins)

❶ *Barbon is recorded in the* Domesday Book *as 'Berebrune' and means a stream frequented by bears or beavers.*

(🏃) After lunch turn left down the road and out of the village. At the junction at Hodge Bridge turn right over the bridge and then left over the gate into the golf course at the footpath sign. Follow the path round next to the river and then head right to the corner of the wall on your right under the overhead power lines. Go through the gap and turn immediately right onto the path between the bushes. This path obviously used to be continuous through the bushes but now has gaps in it where the golf course cuts across. Follow the path uphill through a small wood and soon it emerges again onto the fairway so keep an eye open for little white balls flying through the air. Carry straight on past a holly tree all on its own, and on again to find the path between the bushes once more. Follow this down to a junction and turn left, pass Beckfoot Farm and go over the beck by the concrete bridge, noticing the packhorse bridge on your left. You then pass by Low Beckfoot Farm, go under the old railway bridge and follow the road round to the left and then after about 100 yards go through the five-barred gate on your right with a signpost pointing to Casterton. Follow the fence on your right-hand side, through a gate on your right and then follow the wall on your left. Where the wall ends carry straight on across the field to the step stile over the wall ahead and then head up the field making for the left-hand corner of the wood ahead. Go over the stile and bear left uphill towards the small clump of trees with the slope down on your right towards the woods. Carry on round the slope and then at The Grange go through the gate on your right, with the farm buildings on your left, and then through another gate and follow the track down. At the bottom turn left through a gate and up to the stone barn and carry on with the hedge on your left, over which is the school

Casterton Church at the centre of the village.

playing field. As you approach the stone buildings go through the gate and carry straight on and between them, down some steps and then at the bottom turn left up to the road. Cross over to the Old Vicarage and follow the path at the back of the church and then left again. Follow the lane past the school and under the bridge.

❶ *Casterton School was established in 1823 as The Clergy Daughters' School with benefits confined to the daughters of the clergy with the smallest incomes.*

⍝ At the crossroads go straight over and up the lane opposite with the 'no through road' sign to Langthwaite. The lane becomes grassy after the farm, go through the gate and then at the next gate go right and follow the path through three fields with the wall on your right. It gradually rises up and you follow the wall until you see a gap in the wall, just past where the spring emerges, go left up this field to the gate and into the green lane known as Fellfoot Road where you turn to the right.

❶ *As you walk along this lane look out for the sheepfolds with boulders on either side, over the walls These peculiar constructions were built in 1996 by a man called Andy Goldsworthy with an Cumbria County Council grant of many thousands of pounds. The project, which he* *conceived, will ultimately see the construction of 100 such sheepfolds throughout Cumbria. Why, is anyone's guess but I'm sure someone will give you a good reason, not least Goldsmith himself who says, '... the British landscape is made rich by the relationship between people and the land', and who can argue with that? There are about 12 of them altogether along Fellfoot road and the artist has become quite well known world-wide for his outdoor artistry.*

(🏃) Where the lane exits onto the road you should find your car waiting for you. (4.2 miles; 1 hr 40 mins)

(ⓘ) *The walk Barbondale to Casterton follows the same route but in the opposite direction and with a different lunch venue. Do walk them both, perhaps in different seasons, since they are totally different because all the views change. What doesn't change, of course, are the 'megaliths'!*

Walk 7

Clawthorpe to Burton via Hutton Roof

Outdoor Leisure map 7:   *The English Lakes SE Area*
Distance: 10.3 miles   Walking time: 4 hrs 5 mins
Start at Clawthorpe, Saxton Hagg, grid ref. SD535777
Lunch at *The Kings Arms*, 01524 781409

T HIS WALK starts and finishes in Cumbria but you do
walk into Lancashire and then quickly out of it again.
It involves a certain amount of ascent but nothing to worry
about. It is a varied walk that takes in the rugged, limestone
Hutton Roof Crags and the towpath of the now defunct part
of the Lancaster Canal, as well as the countryside to be
found on the fringes of the Lake District. Burton-in-Kendal
is an unspoilt village boasting at least two pubs and a café.

(🚶) Park the car on a convenient roadside verge and walk up the hill
on the road for about a mile and just where the road starts to
drop downhill go over the stile in the wall on your right.

(ℹ) *You are now walking along part of the Limestone Link footpath which
starts in Arnside and goes through to Kirkby Lonsdale. This is a very
pleasant walk of about 14 miles and can be enjoyed by walking to
Kirkby for an overnight stop and then walking back the following day.*

(🚶) Follow the path round below the limestone of Hutton Roof Crags,
keeping the wall quite near on your left. Eventually you drop
down left to the village of Hutton Roof, passing down between
some rather dramatic limestone outcrops.

(ℹ) *Here the observant will notice that the geology changes quite dramatically
and you have left limestone country and the dominant rock is now
millstone grit.*

(🚶) Turn right along the lane for about 150 yards and then right
again at Low House where you follow the track up through a field.
At the first gate go over and bear slightly to the right and upwards
until you go over a stile right next to the woods and into another

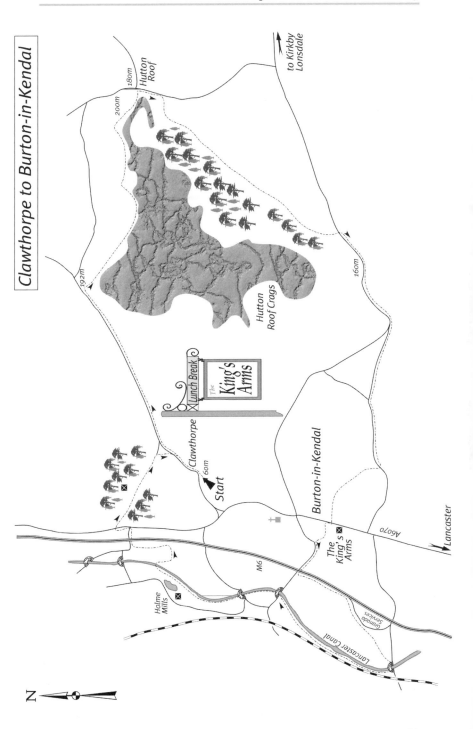

The once-busy road through Burton-in-Kendal.

field. Carry straight on and then follow the boundary of the woods till you come to Crag House. This path can be a little indistinct but don't be put off. Go through the yard and left down to the road. Turn right and follow it for over a mile and then turn right off the road just past the attractively maintained Home Farm, which appears to specialise in horses. Climb up about 20 yards and over the stile in the corner then bear slightly left uphill, over another stile, and bear left again across the field go over another stile into another field and bear left again across to the opposite corner. Here go over a stile into the green lane which takes you to Burton for lunch at *The Kings Arms.* (6.2 miles; 2 hrs 25 mins)

ⓘ *Nowadays Burton appears to be a very ordinary, but nonetheless attractive, village. However, it has a long history and is noted as 'Bortun' in the* Domesday Book. *It was granted a market in 1661 and became the most extensive corn market in Westmorland. However, after the construction of the canal in 1819 the market began to decline. The Lancaster to Kendal turnpike passed through the village but with the coming of the railway the village became even less important. The church of St Chad dates from the thirteenth century and was thoroughly repaired and restored in 1844, having undergone much work during the interim centuries.*

⍟ Turn left out of the pub along Main Street/Boon Walks and left again down Tan Pits Lane. After about half a mile and immediately over the motorway bridge there is a stile on your left with the

A canal bridge on the abandoned Lancaster Canal. The water would originally have been up to the lip just below the path.

pathway alongside the fence. Follow this and eventually you come to the service station on your left. Follow the signs on to Yealand Bridge road where you turn right and go over the border in to Lancashire and to the canal bridge. Go down onto the towpath and head north, or left, alongside the rather sad-looking remains of the canal.

This section of the canal was detached from the southern parts of the Lancaster Canal when the M6 was constructed in the 1960s; an act of destruction which would never be condoned these days and all to save a rather small sum of money. At this time a rather exciting plan has been unfurled to reconnect this stretch and I do hope the plans come to fruition.

After about half a mile you are back in Cumbria again, and a mile further on, just past Holme Mills down on your left, go over the bridge and to the other side of the canal. Turn up the track and left at the top and out onto the road. Turn right to go over the motorway once more and then left at the next junction, immediately crossing over to go over the stile into the field, or more correctly a park. Turn right and follow the path in a straight line crossing over the entrance drive leading to Curwen House. Carry on past the tennis court and into the top corner of the field where you go over a stile into a lane, past some houses and out onto the road. Turn right downhill and back to your car. (4.1 miles; 1 hr 40 mins)

Walk 8

Cockerham to Conder Green

Explorer map 296:   Lancaster, Morecambe
& Fleetwood

Distance: 9.8 miles   Walking time: 3 hrs 45 mins

Start at Village Hall car park, grid ref. SD465521

Lunch at *The Stork*, 01524 751234

THIS IS A GOOD WALK to test out your 'walkability'. It is almost entirely along flat ground just above sea level and it isn't too long. It also has some stretches through fields and over stiles so if you can cope with this walk you could then proceed on to a slightly longer one, perhaps with more ascents – Walk 18, Conder Green to Galgate, perhaps. Do be warned: the paths across the fields can be quite boggy after wet weather. Indeed, most of it was marsh until the monks arrived at Cockersand!

🚶 Leave the car park and take the path to the right of the hall as you stand with your back to the road. Pass through the churchyard and then go through the gate and turn right across the field to the road. Through the gate turn left and follow the road for about 200 yards till you take the footpath on your right. This path goes through about three fields before emerging near to the parachuting centre. Go through the big double gate on your right and then left alongside the beck. Soon you turn left over a footbridge and then another one, also on your right, hidden amongst the trees. Cross this and then go over a stile where you bear left and up to the embankment. Go over onto this and down where you turn right and follow the track until it comes to the road.

❶ *You are now walking along The Lancashire Coastal Path which you will follow as far as Conder Green.*

🚶 Bear left here and follow the embankment to Bank End and then follow the track round the coast with the caravan sites on your right. Eventually you come to Bank Houses and you carry on

Cockerham to Conder Green

Lunch Break

The Stork

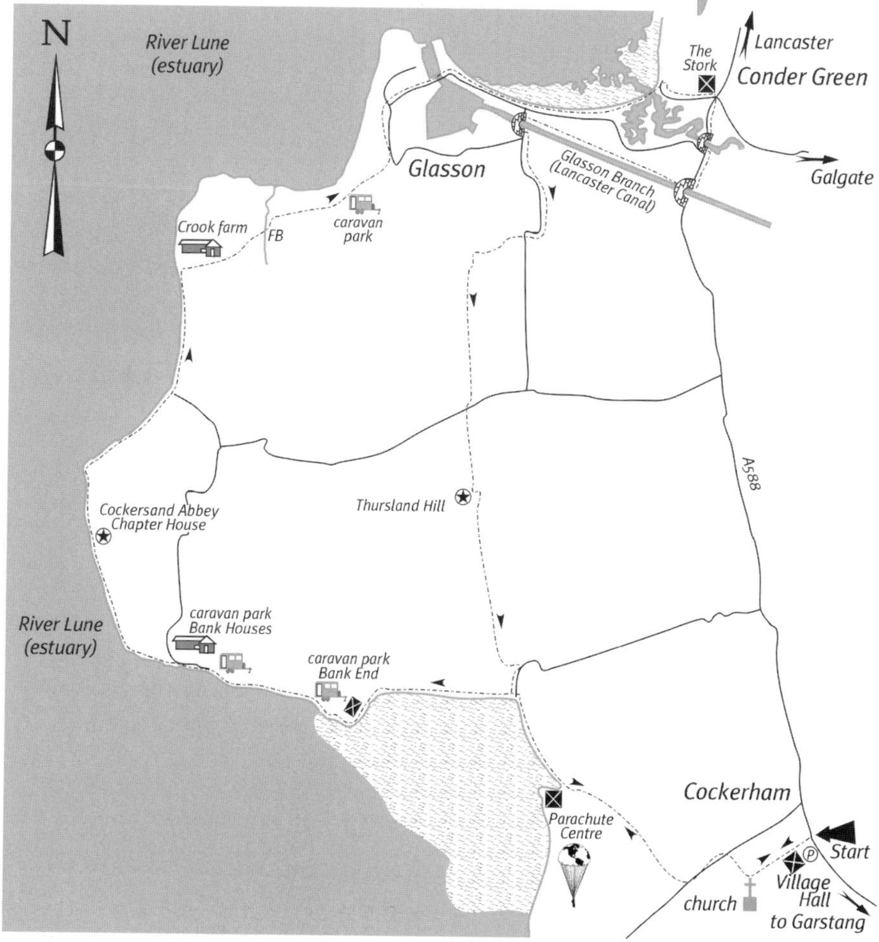

N

River Lune (estuary)

The Stork

Lancaster

Conder Green

Glasson

Glasson Branch (Lancaster Canal)

Galgate

Crook farm   FB

caravan park

Cockersand Abbey Chapter House

Thursland Hill

A588

caravan park Bank Houses

caravan park Bank End

River Lune (estuary)

Parachute Centre

Cockerham

Start

P

Village Hall

church

to Garstang

The Chapter House, Cockersand Abbey, with the Plover Scar lighthouse just visible on the right.

following the path with the sea or salt marsh down on your left. The path is now elevated and it can be quite splendid looking out towards Morecambe Bay and the mouth of the Lune.

This is a sandy coastline with abundant amounts of sandstone just below you, as you will see if the tide is out. At any time of the year you are likely to see oystercatchers scavenging in the sandflats and in winter a rich variety of water and wading birds: great crested grebe, cormorant, grey heron, knot, redshank, to name but a few.

After walking for about 5 minutes you come to the remains of Cockersand Abbey over on your right.

The only remnant of the abbey is the chapter house, where the bodies of the monks were interred, and so escaped destruction, unlike the rest of the buildings. It is one of the few remaining octagonal structures of its type and after the Dissolution it came into the hands of the Catholic

Dalton family from the nearby Thurnham Hall. They in turn interred their dead in the chapter house prior to the building of a church near to the Hall in the nineteenth century. In 1180 Hugh de Garth had a hermitage on the site which he developed into a hospice for lepers. Ten years later monks from the Premonstratensian order in Leicester arrived and it soon became a prosperous abbey with extensive lands throughout north Lancashire and Westmorland. For years the white-robed brethren toiled at the task of building their abbey, the church being dedicated to St Mary. Like many others it was dissolved on the orders of Henry VIII. Much of the stone and internal fittings, including the windows, found their way into other buildings in the area, the choir stalls in Lancaster Priory being but one example.

🏃 Carrying on you will soon arrive at Plover Hill (so named, I suspect, because it is ever so slightly higher than the rest of the surrounding land and was popular with plovers) and further on the old Abbey Lighthouse where you get onto a decent track.

ℹ️ *The Plover Scar lighthouse was erected in 1843 out on the edge of the saltmarsh to mark the entrance to the Lune channel and over on the opposite shore the remote habitation of Sunderland Point. The building where the Abbey Lighthouse was still stands but looks rather sad at the time of writing.*

🏃 Carry on along what is now a good track until Crook Farm where you turn right and go away from the coast. Follow the path through the fields and over the bridge and then turn left past the caravan park, through a gate and on up onto the road. Turn left and at the next junction take the left fork and into Glasson.

ℹ️ *The dock was opened in 1787 and at the time was capable of containing 25 merchantmen. It was the construction of this dock which effectively meant the end of Sunderland Point as a port. The lock gates which maintain a constant level of water were at the time of its construction something unusual. The adjoining canal basin was constructed in 1825 and facilitated access to the Lancaster Canal via the 2½-mile Glasson branch canal. This canal basin was capable of containing ships of '500 tons burthen', which meant that the merchantmen could unload directly onto the canal barges. The dock still operates commercially and it is likely you will see at least one small coaster plying the Isle of Man route being loaded or unloaded. The canal basin is now mainly given over to pleasure craft.*

Glasson Dock.

Glasson canal basin.

(🚶) Go over the swing bridge and at the toilets go down the right hand side to the path, turn right and follow the old railway track along the coast, though when the tide is out, as it mostly, is it may be difficult to believe this is the coast. After almost a mile, and having gone over a bridge, turn right and follow this road to Conder Green and *The Stork Inn.* (5.6 miles; 2 hrs)

(🚶) As you leave the pub go straight down the road opposite until you come to the canal bridge where you go down onto the towpath and follow it in the direction of Glasson. Leave it at the bridge just before you get to Glasson and go to the right over the bridge, following the road south but carrying straight on where it bends round to the right. This lane bends first to the left and then right and after about 300 yards it bends right and then left. Just at the left-hand bend go over the stile on your right and follow the fence on your right. At the end of the field the fence goes left and you keep on following it until it bears right, but you bear left and south with a ditch on your right. Over a footbridge and straight on you eventually come out onto the road by a small barn or hut. It could be tricky here since the two gates were locked when we passed by, even though it is a public footpath. Cross over the lane and over the stile into another field which you cross with the fence on your left. You then go over two rather tricky stiles and into another field. Head towards the Thursland Hall farm across this field and as you approach the farm go over a stile and then through the gate on your left and round the fence of the farm garden on your right. Follow the path south again with the fence on your right and after about 1,000 yards (15 mins) the path bends left and you come out onto the road. Turn right and follow it back to the place where you turned left for Bank End earlier in the day. The rest is simple since you retrace your steps through the parachuting centre and over the fields back to Cockerham. (4.2 miles; 1 hr 45 mins)

Walk 9

Conder Green to Galgate

Explorer map 296:   Lancaster, Morecambe
                      & Fleetwood
Distance: 9.2 miles   Walking time: 3 hrs 20 mins
Start Conder Green picnic site, grid ref. SD 457561
Lunch at *The Plough Inn*, 01524 751337

A GOOD WINTER WALK, or one after wet weather, since this follows reasonably good footpaths all the way. It starts going north along the old railway line from Glasson to Lancaster and then via the canal towpaths of the Lancaster Canal and the Glasson branch. These can be hard work, since some stretches are not well maintained but at least they're flat. Absolutely no hills. Well, just one little one of about 50 yards.

🚶 The picnic site is at the end of the narrow lane which passes the front of *The Stork Inn* at Conder Green and which used to be the site of a railway station on the Glasson to Lancaster line. Having parked your car and secured it safely set off north up the path away from the direction you have arrived and which is part of the Lancashire Coastal Way.

ℹ️ *Over on your left is the River Lune but you can't really see it at first and when it does appear you have wonderful views of the distant Lake District on a good day, and also over the Lune estuary and its myriad water birds, especially in winter. Across the river is Overton, among the trees, and Bazil Point, from where at one time a ferry used to cross over to Glasson. The railway line was built in 1887 by The London and North Western Railway Co., and linked Glasson with Lancaster. The station at Conder Green was opened in 1890 and became disused in 1930 when passenger services along the line ceased. The line finally closed in 1964.*

🚶 After about 30 minutes, depending on whether or not you have dawdled, you will have walked the 1½ miles to the point where

50

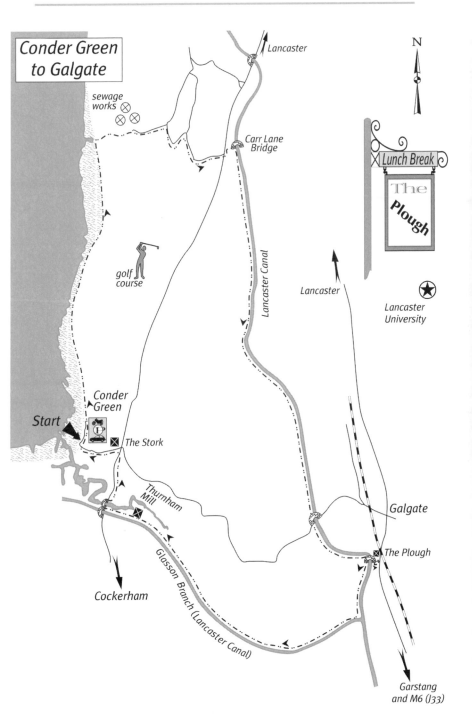

Conder Green
to Galgate

Lancaster

N

sewage
works

Carr Lane
Bridge

Lunch Break

The
Plough

golf
course

Lancaster Canal

Lancaster

Lancaster
University

Conder
Green

Start

The Stork

Thurnham
Mill

Galgate

The Plough

Cockerham

Glasson Branch (Lancaster Canal)

Garstang
and M6 (J33)

The 'turnover' bridge where the Glasson branch meets the Lancaster Canal.

you leave the path. Turn right down a track which leads you past the sewage works over on your left and then onto a narrow lane. Take the first turning on your right, up another narrow lane, which goes up a little and then bends to the left. You're soon at a T junction so turn right, having gone past a water pump which does work, and Grange Farm will be on your right. Follow this lane for about another 350 yards and you arrive at another T junction but this time it is quite a busy road so do be careful. Cross over and turn left to the footpath sign and then down the short track to the canal bridge. Turn right through the stile and down to the towpath of the Lancaster Canal and turn right, or south.

ⓘ *This is Carr Lane bridge and is numbered 93 and this is just one of four bridges along the stretch of the canal known as the Deep Cutting, for reasons which I am sure are obvious. The cutting starts about half a mile to the north at bridge 94 where Ashton Road crosses over the canal.*

Soon the forbidding atmosphere of the cutting opens out to views across pastures which can be rich in birdlife, especially herons, and gradually houses on the outskirts of Galgate are approached.

❶ *Having passed Ellel Hall bridge (No. 88) about 200 yards further on you will go over the 'Conder aqueduct'; lean over carefully to to see the stream hurrying beneath the low arch and enjoy the splendid buttresses and curved walls, marvelling at the architectural detail of what is really a very ordinary piece of engineering but still an outstanding example of John Rennie's design.*

⚲ After walking for about an hour, or 2½ miles, you will arrive opposite Galgate and you have to go up from the towpath and over the bridge (No. 86) out onto the A6. Just before this bridge you will notice a café opposite across the canal. Turn left at the road and after about 50 yards you will find *The Plough Inn* where you can stop for lunch. (5.7 miles; 2 hrs)

⚲ Leaving the pub you retrace your steps back to the canal towpath and continue south until you come to the junction with the Glasson branch.

❶ *Here there is a 'turnover bridge', which is so named because the horses drawing the canal boats could change from one towpath to the other without being unhitched. This would save time and just like today, 'time is money'. This would have been particularly important to the packet-boat owners who guaranteed swift passage. If you have time you will be able to study the bridge and work out for yourself how it worked. Here is also a lock, one of six along the branch canal, as the waterway climbs from sea level at Glasson to the height of 25 metres (82 ft), which is of course the height above sea level of the entire length of the Lancaster Canal as it is today. The Lancaster Canal is unique in England, there being no locks whatsoever from Tewitfield to Preston. The Glasson branch opened in December 1825, some 28 years after the stretch of the Lancaster Canal from Preston to Tewitfield saw its first barge.*

⚲ So, having lingered long enough, set off westwards towards Glasson along a towpath which is unusual in these parts since it is not entirely flat. It descends as you pass by each lock.

❶ *As you pass by the third lock bridge look over the canal towards the church spire sticking up above the trees. This is the Roman Catholic*

The junction of the Glasson branch with the Lancaster canal showing the locks and the 'turnover' bridge.

church of St Thomas and St Elizabeth, designed by Charles Hansom, opened in 1848 and founded by the pious and benevolent Miss Elizabeth Dalton. To its right you may just espy the Gothic façade of Thurnham Hall, the ancient seat of the Dalton family, descendants of St Thomas More. This is now a holiday time-share development, the last of the family having moved out in 1983.

(🏃) In just under an hour, or after 2¼ miles, you will go under a bridge and you will see the marina, or inner dock, about 300 yards in front of you. Leave the towpath here and go up to the road, but take care since the bridge is quite narrow and vehicles may catch you unawares. Here you turn left and walk down to the T junction. Cross over and bear left for 20 yards before going across the grass on your right and onto the path. Once again this is the old railway line, now part of the Lancashire Coastal Way on which you set off earlier. Turn right and follow the path to your car, enjoying the views of the estuary and its intricate network of creeks as you go. (3.5 miles; 1 hr 20 mins)

Walk 10

Crook o' Lune to Hest Bank

Outdoor Leisure Map 41:   Forest of Bowland & Ribblesdale
Distance: 10.4 miles.   Walking time: 4 hrs 20 mins
Start at Crook o' Lune car park, grid ref. SD522647
Lunch at *The Hest Bank Inn*, 01524 824339

T HIS WALK begins by going downstream along the Lune, then along a green lane and a short stretch of road through a caravan site, and more road to Hest Bank for lunch. The return is along the canal towpath and then up the old railway line back to Crook o' Lune. So most of the walk is flat, apart from the short section through the caravan site, and reasonably firm under foot too.

(🏃) Leaving the car park go down the steps to the old railway line and turn right under the stone road bridge and then over the metal bridge across the Lune. At the far side take the riverside path right and follow it along the bank and through the trees until the weir.

(ℹ) *Just here there is an intake for North West Water's Lancashire Conjunctive Use Scheme. This enables up to 62 million gallons of water a day to be taken from the river to be pumped into the water supply system of the north west of England.*

(🏃) Go over the stile and left up the steps to the path and turn right and up back onto the old railway line. Follow this to the old railway station and there cross over the narrow bulk bridge to Halton. Turn left at *The Greyhound* and walk into the village keeping to the left-hand pavement. At the crossroads keep left again.

(ℹ) *As you walk down the slope, up on your right is Castle Hill with a flag pole atop. This is a Norman motte and bailey. The church of St Wilfrid stands on a pre-conquest site. It was rebuilt in 1792 and any remains of its great age was veiled by a reconstruction during the 1870s. The tower is perpendicular and in the churchyard you will find*

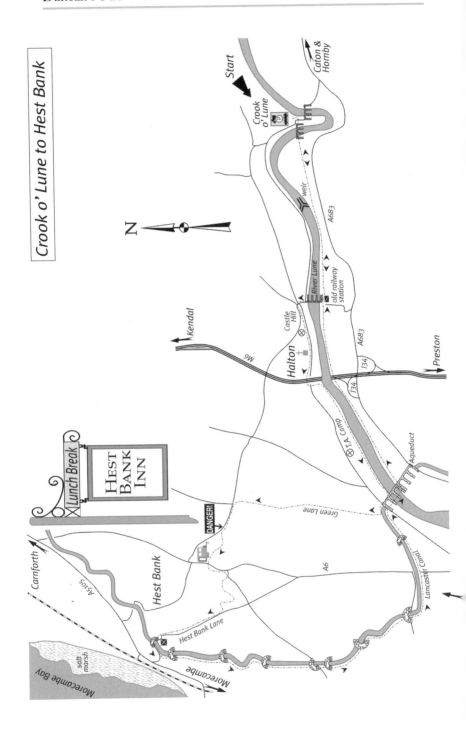

Crook o' Lune to Hest Bank

The motte and bailey at Halton.

The 'restored' Celtic cross at Halton.

a tall, tapering Anglo-Scandinavian eleventh-century cross bearing both Christian and pagan symbols. Sadly the Victorians added a head to the cross, to replace the lost original, but that in itself is of historical value, if only to show that throughout the ages people have erected or added unsuitable architectural features when totally unnecessary or inappropriate.

🚶 Soon you will go under the motorway where you immediately go left over a stile and onto a path leading down towards the river. Eventually you pass by a TA camp up on your right and keeping close to the river bank you soon pass into some trees and go under the Lune aqueduct soaring above you. You will cross this on your return journey. Follow the path up and you emerge onto the canal towpath. Turn left and immediately go up the slope by the road bridge and then over it, taking care to watch out for vehicles. Immediately on your left over the bridge drop down to a stile on your left and follow the path beside the fence on your left. This curves round by a small copse and soon you will come to a stile over which you turn right and follow the track which is known as 'Green lane'. After one mile this meets with Bottomdale road and you turn left here. Do take care the road is quite busy and although you are only on it for about 400 yards it is dangerous for walkers.

ⓘ *When walking along a road you should, of course, walk in single file and keep to the right hand side so that you face oncoming traffic; and you should be ready at all times to dive sideways into the hedge!*

🚶 On this stretch you are going downhill and with a right hand bend in front of you, therefore it is wisest to keep to the left on this occasion, since at the right hand bend you cross over to take to a footpath on the left. However, you are doing the walking, so make your own decision, but do take care. Go over the stile and through a short field before going over a stile into a caravan site. Go straight ahead and up the road ahead, there is a sign indicating the footpath and as you go up the slope bear left to follow the wall and up, with a caravan on your right. Go through the gate and with the hedge on your left carry on up and then at the crest go down keeping to the left. You go over another stile and then down a short path, past a house on your right, and out onto the road. This is the A6 and on your right is *Slyne Lodge* hotel. Cross

over and turn left and then first right down Throstle Grove. At
the first bend there is a path on your right which goes down
between a house and the drive into Slyne House retirement home.
Soon you're on Throstle walk, so turn left and then at the junction
left again along Manor Road. Then after 200 yards right into
Warren Drive. At the top turn left along Bay View crescent and
then right again at the junction with Hest Bank lane. Follow this
for about 600 yards and you will arrive at the *Hest Bank Inn.* (5.4
miles; 2 hrs) There's usually a good selection of bar meals and
snacks here, as well as a good range of beers. In the days when
the canal was in use for commercial traffic this was a popular
hostelry for the boatmen.

🚶 Leaving the pub, turn left and go over the canal bridge and then
down the steps to the canal towpath. Turn right and follow the
path for 2.4 miles, about an hour.

ⓘ *Before the coming of the railway in the mid-nineteenth century Hest
Bank was the starting point, from time immemorial, for the coach and
horses route across the sands to Furness, from whence they would travel
up the coast of what is now Cumbria and onwards to Carlisle and
Scotland. So important was it that the Monarch appointed an official
guide, a post which is still held and at the time of writing his name
is Cedric Robinson. A number of times each year he leads large groups
across the sands and you may wish to try this walk out sometime. The
only trouble is that the pub is at the other side and you can't walk
back! Since the canal preceded the railway by almost 50 years it is most
probable that these coaches will have picked up passengers who had
travelled north on the canal packet boats. Indeed during the early days
of the canal goods were transported downhill to the shore and put
aboard coasters for transhipment to Ireland, North Wales, Barrow and
Scotland. The opening of the Glasson branch in 1825 put an end to
this practice. Over on your right you will see Morecambe and Morecambe
Bay and with luck you will also have a grand view over to the Furness
peninsula. Walking along the towpath you will see quite a few birds
and as you near Lancaster keep an eye out for kingfishers darting from
overhanging branch to branch.*

🚶 Having gone under bridge 108, over which you passed on the
outward journey, you will find yourself going over the River Lune
on the aqueduct under which you passed earlier.

The canal at Hest Bank.

❶ *The aqueduct was built by Alexander Stevens & Son of Edinburgh to John Rennie's design in 1797 and you will no doubt marvel at its excellence. The aqueduct is 664 ft long and stands 60 ft above the river. Four piers support the five arches, one of which is on the south bank and under which you will soon pass. Sadly the cost of this construction, £48,321 against the original estimate of £27,500, was so great that when they came to build another further south in Preston across the Ribble, to join the Lancaster Canal to the Leeds & Liverpool Canal at an estimated cost of £180,195, the directors decided on a wagonway instead. It was a sensible decision but it meant that the canal was cut off from the rest of England's waterways. This isolation remained for over 200 years until in 2002 a link was built from the canal to the Ribble from where vessels could gain access to the Leeds & Liverpool Canal via the River Douglas. If only the engineers had thought of this way back in the eighteenth century it is almost certain that the northern end leading up to Kendal wouldn't have been cut in the 1960s during the construction of the M6.*

❄ You will no doubt have taken a look at the view from the viaduct and once you have crossed over you drop down the steps on your right and then right again to go under and follow the old railway line north. Despite what it says on the signpost it is only 2½ miles to Crook O'Lune.

John Rennie's aqueduct over the River Lune

ℹ️ *The railway line was opened in 1850 running from Lancaster to Wennington where it joined the Skipton to Carnforth line. It was known as the 'Little' North Western Railway so it wouldn't be confused with the London North Western. One of the Directors of the company was Edmund Sharp who later bought Halton Hall, now all but demolished. He was responsible for the purchase of rolling stock which on delivery was found to be unsuitable in a variety of ways; the prime one being that it was too wide for the line, which at its opening wasn't the standard gauge! Passenger services stopped in 1965. It was upgraded into a splendid cycle route during 2000 with a 'Millennium Fund' grant.*

🚶 Follow the path eastwards alongside the river, down on your left, for another 2.5 miles, or about an hour, back to Crook o' Lune and your car. (5.5 miles; 2 hrs)

If Woody's mobile café is there you will be able to have a cup of tea and drink in the memorable view of the Lune Valley, as captured by the English Victorian watercolourist J. M. W. Turner.

Walk 11

Crook o' Lune to Hornby

Outdoor Leisure Map 41:   Forest of Bowland
& Ribblesdale

Distance: 11 miles.   Walking time: 4 hrs 50 mins

Start at Crook o' Lune car park, grid ref. SD 522647

Lunch at *The Royal Oak*, 015242 61344

THIS IS A GOOD RAMBLE and relatively flat, other than for one of two very short ascents along the footpath going east. These are through the woods and it is not so much the gradient as the slipperiness in wet weather that causes any difficulty. Crossing the Lune at Loyn Bridge and then into Hornby the return is alongside the southerly bank of the Lune and is very flat. The last mile is along the old railway line back to the start where you will usually find a good cup of tea and a scone at Woody's mobile café.

(⚐) Descend the steps from the car park down to the north bank of the Lune and set off up river in a north easterly direction, upstream all the way to Loyn Bridge. The path is clearly marked all the way, being the Lune Valley Ramble. After a mile you go under the viaduct carrying water from Thirlmere to Manchester.

ⓘ *This is the only point on its 88-mile journey where you can walk under the pipes and only one of about four places it actually surfaces.*

(⚐) Soon you enter the woods and after about 400 yards you go down and over a stile into a field. Turn sharp left, unless you want to follow the official route and a big loop in the river, following the fence of Burton Woods (managed by Lancashire Wildlife Trust) on your left. As you approach a fence bear to the right a little and go through a gate (If you've followed the loop this is where you meet up with the other path) and follow the track to Aughton Barns.

ⓘ *As a matter of interest just as Claughton, across the river, is pronounced Clafton, Aughton is pronounced Afton.*

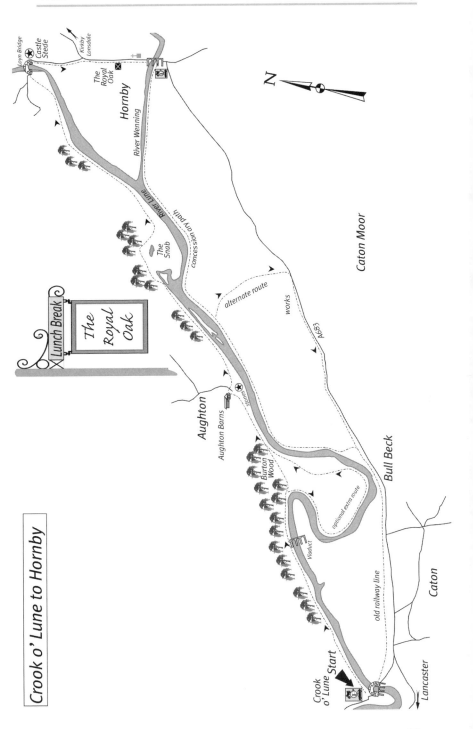

Crook o' Lune to Hornby

Loyn Bridge
Castle Stede
Kirkby Lonsdale
The Royal Oak
Hornby
River Wenning
N
The Snab
River Lune
concession path
Lunch Break
The Royal Oak
alternate route
works
A683
Caton Moor
Aughton
Aughton Barns
Steps
Burton Wood
optional extra route
Viaduct
Bull Beck
old railway line
Caton
Crook o' Lune Start
Lancaster

*One of the megaliths
at Aughton Bottoms,
reputed to be
Norman boundary
stones.*

(🚶) As you turn left in front of the barns take the stile over the fence on your right and across the field to another stile.

(ℹ️) *In this field there are a number of 'megaliths', which look like grave headstones and are seemingly placed at random. If you look carefully you will see they are mostly in two lines at right angles to each other appearing to be all that remains of a 'slab wall'. More probably they are the remnant of a boundary which is almost definitely Norman and probably goes back much earlier than that.*

(🚶) Go through two more fields and then the path is alongside the river again passing through Great Close wood, with islets on your right, before emerging into the open again and close by the river bank before more trees and bushes and through another field to The Snab. Turn right down the track and left round the corner and then take the right hand fork down to a gate and out along the flat river plain. Carry on with the fence on your left and not turning up to the entrance to Sandbeds Farm carry on, up a grassy bank and through some more trees before entering a big field where in the distance you can see Loyn Bridge. There go through the gap in the wall onto the road and turn right over the bridge.

(ℹ️) *As you cross the bridge, built in 1684, and turn right uphill towards Hornby, above the bank of trees on the left is the site of Castle Stede, a Norman motte and bailey, and this also shows signs of being older, probably Saxon.*

(🚶) Carry on up to the junction and straight ahead and on into Hornby where, just past the school, is *The Royal Oak* where you can stop for lunch. (5.7 miles; 2 hrs 30 mins)

ⓘ *Hornby is an ancient habitation, being a strategic site on the old main road north to Scotland. Even as recently as 1974 it had its own magistrates' court and until the local government reorganisation of the same year was the administrative centre of the Lunesdale Rural District Council. There has been a castle here since just after the Norman Conquest and it is reputed that a Roman villa was on the same site. At the Conquest a man named Alric was in possession of Hornby and his granddaughter married Adam, Nicholas or Roger Montbegon, all the same person. (There is no clear documentary evidence of his first name, though it would seem Adam is the favourite.) It was he who built the original castle here. The large square tower, or keep, was the creation of Sir Edward Stanley, the first Lord Mounteagle, created a peer following his success in battle at Flodden Field. The imposing present-day castle with its Gothic towers is more recent having been added in 1848. The church of St Margaret is also interesting; the octagonal tower having been added by Sir Edward as fulfilment of a vow in honour of his patron saint and having returned victorious from Scotland. Inscribed on the face of the tower you will find, 'E. Stanley miles Dns Monteagle me fieri fecit' which translated says, 'Edward Stanley Lord Monteagle had me built.' There are also the remains of some interesting ninth-century crosses in the church porch. One of these has the five loaves and two fishes and is unique in England. In the churchyard is the stump of a cross which must have been at least 12 feet high in its entirety. Across the road is the Catholic Presbytery of St Mary where in the early part of the nineteenth century lived a much loved and learned priest, Dr John Lingard, who wrote his famous 'History of England'. There is a tablet in his memory across the road in the Anglican church, which at the time was a most unusual deed but proves the tolerance and good nature of north Lancashire folk where religion is involved.*

🚶 After lunch turn right and carry on through the village, past *The County Hotel* where you can also have lunch if you choose, over the bridge and sharp right into a car park. Then slip through the gap in the wall next to the bridge and turn left following the River Wenning down on your right. After about 800 yards the public footpath turns away from the river but you can carry on along the river following a concessionary path which eventually brings you to the confluence of the Wenning and the Lune where the path turns west, or to the left.

❶ *This stretch of river is popular with water birds who obviously find its clean waters a good hunting ground; probably to the annoyance of the many anglers who also favour this stretch. You may well spot a wide range, depending on the time of the year, but it is a favourite with oystercatchers, common sandpipers, wagtails, herons, coots and a variety of ducks and swans. Also in winter flocks of Canada geese rest on the flood plain, together with fieldfare and redwing; not forgetting curlew, who have made the short trip down from the fells for the winter. Across the river, under the overhanging trees and bushes, you may glimpse the iridescent blue flash of a kingfisher as it darts from favourite perch to favourite perch.*

⊛ Then you simply walk alongside the Lune for about 2 miles until the river comes near to the road and some trees at Bull Beck.

WARNING

After leaving the conjunction of the Wenning and the Lune the concessionary path joins up with a Public Right of Way again but at the time of writing there is a notice here warning you that the footpath ahead is closed. The reason is that the footpath has been washed away by the river and the owner of the land will not let anyone walk over his land. He is very firm about this and will likely come out to meet you and order you to return. It is understood that discussions are taking place in the hope that a concessionary path may be opened but until then you will have to turn, left, away from the river. Follow the path to the road at Claughton and then turn right to follow the road as far as Bull Beck, where you can turn to the right and walk back to Crook o' Lune along the old railway line.

⊛ Climb up onto the old railway line and turn right following the path for about 1½ miles back to Crook o' Lune. (5.3 miles; 2 hrs 20 mins)

If you do decide on a mug of tea from Woody's mobile Café (with real mugs) and it is a nice day you won't find a finer spot to sit and drink it as you look up the Lune in the direction of where you set off earlier. In the distance is Hornby Castle and behind it Ingleborough. One of England's finest views and captured for eternity by Turner.

Walk 12

Crook o' Lune to Over Kellet

Outdoor Leisure Map 41:   Forest of Bowland & Ribblesdale
Distance: 10.5 miles   Walking time: 4 hrs 15 mins
Start at Crook o' Lune car park, grid ref. SD 522647
Lunch at *The Eagle's Head*, 01524 732457

MUCH OF THE OUTWARD WALK is across fields, and for a mile or two is alongside the Lune. Apart from the short, sharp 90 metre (295 ft) ascent up to Aughton Church from the Lune Valley the going is relatively gentle, though the fields can be hard going after wet weather. The return is mainly along good paths and quiet lanes.

Despite the warning notices about car thieves, this is a good place to park a car. There's usually someone about whose car is also parked and of course Woody will probably be there with his splendid refreshment van.

Set off by walking down the path beside the wooden picnic tables and drop down to the riverside walk and head east, up river with the Lune down on your right-hand side.

The view you enjoy as you set off was captured by the renowned Victorian landscape artist J. M. W. Turner and if you know the painting, or indeed have a print, you will notice that the view hasn't essentially changed since the mid-nineteenth century.

The path is easy to follow through the riverside pastures, a small stretch of trees, then more pasture and soon you pass under the pipeline through which water flows from Thirlmere to Manchester.

In fact this is one of the few times the pipeline appears above ground in its entire 110-mile or so journey.

The path then passes through more trees before descending down to a stile and over onto the river plain. Bearing left and moving slightly away from the woods you will pick up the path which eventually brings you to Aughton Barns. Here you leave the Lune

Crook o' Lune to Over Kellet

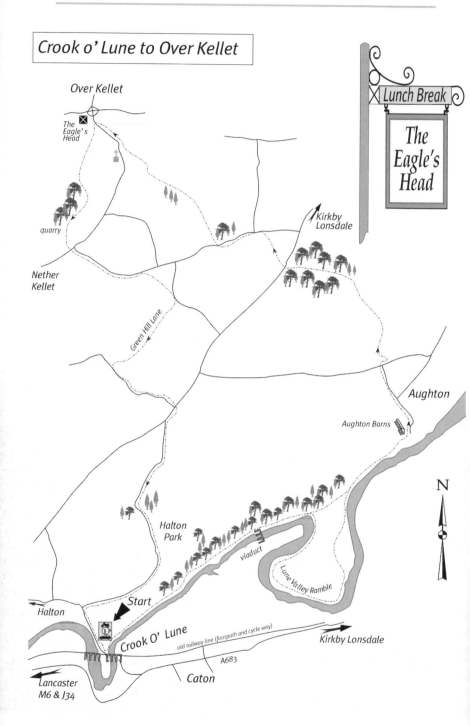

Over Kellet

The Eagle's Head

quarry

Nether Kellet

Green Hill Lane

Kirkby Lonsdale

Aughton

Aughton Barns

Halton Park

viaduct

Lune Valley Ramble

Start

Halton

Crook O' Lune

old railway line (footpath and cycle way)

Kirkby Lonsdale

Caton

A683

Lancaster M6 & J34

Lunch Break

The Eagle's Head

N

Valley Ramble and head up the rather steep lane to the hamlet of Aughton.

ⓘ *This is a very steep lane in which you rise 50 metres (160 ft). One way of making this seem less arduous is trying to spot as many different species of flower on the banks, or during the winter months, the number of species in the hedgerows. I know it doesn't make the hill any less steep but it takes your mind of it! Aughton, pronounced 'Afton', is an ancient village which was at one time an important basket weaving centre, using the willows from the banks of the Lune.*

ⓧ Carry straight on at the crossroads in the centre of Aughton, after which the ascent is more gentle, and then at the top turn right at the T junction. Just opposite the church hall you take the footpath over the stile on your left and head for the next stile straight across the field. Over this you then spot a gate on the skyline so, bearing right, head up the slope towards the gate and

Looking east towards Hornby and Ingleborough from the picnic site at Crook o' Lune: 'Turner's view'

as you approach it you will see that you don't go through this but go over the stile next to the trees. Bear right a bit and you'll spot another stile in the fence and then go up the slope to the very obvious step stile over the hedge on your right. Go over this and bearing right look out for two trees ahead. Go over the stile next to them and then up the field with the hedge on your right and soon you come to a white house. Go over the rather elaborate metal stile and then along the short passage, which can be rather wet, to the next stile and then bear right beside the house and turn left to follow the lane through the trees to the road. Turn left and on your right will be a stile into a field across which you will spot a farmhouse in some trees. Head down the field and through a gate onto a lane. Turn left and straight on at the junction; up this lane is the house you saw from the top of the last field. Just past the entrance to the quarry, on your left, take the footpath over the stile on your right and head down the field. Go through the fence by the gate and then head straight on in the direction of the big tree, to the left of which is another stile. The arrows on the stile point to the right but ignore this since there is another footpath heading straight up the field in the direction of the rectangular copse you will see. Head for the far end of the copse and there is a gap stile into a field. Go through this and follow the hedge on your right. As it drops down there is a stile on your right, it was rather dodgy the last time we went over it, so do take care. Bear left downhill and you will eventually spot a step stile hiding behind a holly bush. Go over this and then head for the big step stile you can see ahead amongst the trees and bushes, just past the collection of farm machinery. Over the step stile scramble round the rocks and then head for the left hand corner of this small field where you then go down a passage on to the road. Bear right and follow the road into the village where you will soon come across the *Eagle's Head* where you can stop for a pint and some lunch. (5.7 miles; 2 hrs 30 mins)

❶ *Over Kellet is yet another ancient village mentioned in the Domesday Book as 'Chellet', from the Norse 'slope with a spring'. Its sister village of Nether Kellet is about 2 miles south down 'the slope' but the where-abouts of the 'spring' is anyone's guess.*

㊟ Leaving the pub turn right and just before the old school take the steps up on your right.

70

The centre of Over Kellet.

ⓘ *The old school was originally endowed by Thomas Wilson in 1677 and known then as 'The Free Grammar School'. In 1973 a new school was built and the building became two private dwellings but happily Thomas Wilson hasn't been forgotten since one of the houses is known as 'Wilson Lodge'.*

🚶 When you emerge into the meadow at the top, head for the right of the old stone barn and then over the stile and go up the next field, with the hedge on your left, and up to the wood. Don't be put off by the warning signs; the path is a right of way, but you shouldn't wander through the woods since you may fall into the quarry. Follow the path through the woods and then it emerges into the stock yard of Leapers Wood quarry where you wander through piles of thermalite blocks. Don't worry, the path is very well marked and you soon come out onto the road. Turn left and then first right up the road sign posted to Kirkby Lonsdale. After the left hand curve in the road and where it starts to climb up take the footpath on your right into the private fishing grounds.

Head left for the gate you can see just below the gorse and the outcrop. Through the gate bear right and then go up left towards the buildings you can just see. A stile leads you out onto the road, where you turn right and go down the green lane which has a sign pointing out it is private property. That may be so but it is a bridle path and so you can walk along it. Follow this to the next junction then turn left, up hill and follow the road to the next junction where you turn right. Despite not facing the oncoming traffic I think it is safer to cross over to the left since, just at the crest of the hill, you take the lane to your left and this is on a rather nasty right hand curve in the road and not a good place to cross over. Please yourself but take care of cars rushing along rather faster than they ought to do. You are now on Park Lane, since it passes Halton Park, and is downhill nearly all the way.

❶ *As you descend you will have a wonderful panoramic view across to Claughton Moor, with its eerie windmills, the Lune Valley, Crook o' Lune and across towards The Ashton Memorial in Williamson Park and parts of Lancaster.*

🚶 Lower down the lane levels off somewhat and passes through open pasture till it comes to the junction with the road to Halton. Turn left and follow the road down hill back to the car park. (4.8 miles; 1 hr 45 mins)

Hindburn Bridge to High Bentham

Outdoor Leisure Map 41: Forest of Bowland & Ribblesdale
Distance: 11.2 miles. Walking time: 4 hrs 50 mins
Start at Hindburn Bridge, grid ref. SD 613676
Lunch at *The Coach House*, 015242 21250

THIS WALK takes you into North Yorkshire for about a
third of the walk. It also takes you through many fields
which can be tough going after wet weather, or in spring
when the grass is high. It also takes you along a delightful
stretch of the River Wenning. There are some good views
east towards the Pennines and northwards towards the
Howgills, up the Lune valley. You also visit the Benthams,
High and Low, which are interesting.

There aren't many places to park a car near to Hindburn Bridge,
in fact there's just room for one small car near to the track where
you start off the walk. However, if you drive about another 150
yards on towards Bentham there's a lay-by on your right with
room for about six cars.

From the bridge walk up the track on your left, indicated by the
footpath sign, and just round the bend there is a stile on your
right; go over it and walk across the field in the direction of the
wall opposite and the next stile. Bearing slightly left head for the
opposite corner of this field and cross over the footbridge. Turn
right and walk along the path with the wood up on your left.
Make for this and through the gate turn right and follow the lane
to the junction. Carry straight on uphill, keeping to the right and
in single file. At the top of the hill you should get a splendid view
which includes Ingleborough. You'll soon pass Four Score Acres
and then Ashleys, where you cross over to the left of the road
since you are taking a footpath on your left and this is found on
a right hand bend in the road, which is not the best place to cross
over. Over the stile go down the field bearing to the right and
heading for the field bridge below. Over the bridge turn left onto

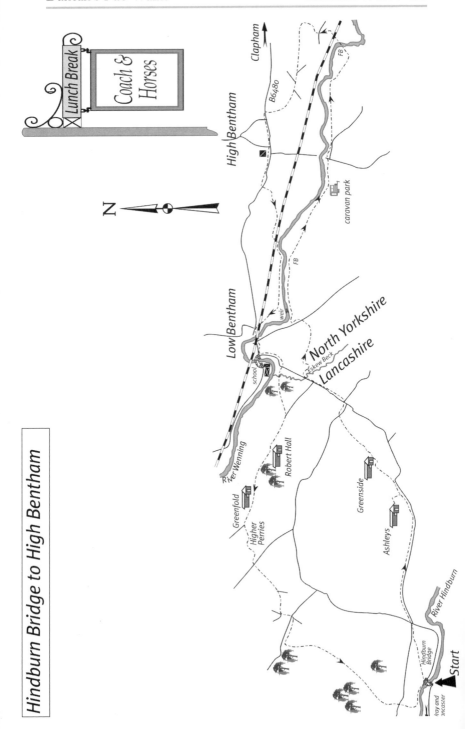

Hindburn Bridge to High Bentham

Lunch Break

Coach & Horses

N

Clapham

B6480

FB

High Bentham

caravan park

FB

Low Bentham

weir

North Yorkshire

Eskew Beck

Lancashire

school

River Wenning

Greenfold

Robert Hall

Higher Perries

Greenside

Ashleys

River Hindburn

Hindburn Bridge

Troy and Lancaster

Start

*The boundary stone
on Eskew Beck
Bridge. Tatham is in
Lancashire and
Bentham is in North
Yorkshire.*

the track and soon you come to Greenside farm. The path here is not clear and it is obvious the farmer does not want to help. Go through the gate on your left and turn right behind the house. This is not the correct route, which goes through the yard, but it is the way the farmer would prefer you to go. Having passed behind the house you walk along the field veering up the slope on your left and then where there used to be a hedge go further up the slope and head towards to the two white houses you should see. The gate into this track will be tied up so you have to climb over it. Go down the track and emerge onto the lane with Hunter's Barn on your left. Turn right and at the next junction turn left and follow this lane gradually down-hill.

❶ *Just over a bridge you leave Lancashire to enter Yorkshire. Eskew Beck, which flows under the bridge, marks the boundary.*

🚶 Turn right up the track to Eskewbeck farm. Go through the yard and straight on through the gate. Move over to your right and follow the hedge down the field and at the bottom turn left and follow this hedge, on your right, down to the gate ahead. Cross straight over the road and over the stile opposite and down to

75

the River Wenning at the bottom. Here you turn right and you
will see a weir.

ⓘ *Across the river look for 'The Cut' or mill-race which at one time fed*
water to Low Bentham mill, built in 1785 to produce wet-spun flax
yarns. The mill has long ceased to function but the race is still used to
supply water to the fish farm ponds you will see on your return journey.
Wenning is from the old English meaning 'dark river'.

(🏃) Follow the path along the river going through two fields. The
path then heads uphill and away from the river and you keep to
the left following the boundary. Over another stile keep your eyes
open and you will see a gate down a slope on your left. Go through
and follow the path which eventually leads you through a caravan
site where you follow the main track and when you see a sign
'Way Out' bear to the right and follow this track which eventually
brings you out by Bentham Bridge.

ⓘ *Here you could simply turn left and follow the road up into High*
Bentham and this will shorten your walk by about 1¾ miles. So if

The town hall,
High Bentham.

you're tired or it is not a very nice day you may wish to take this option.

(🏃) If you wish to do the whole walk, just cross over and follow the lane opposite. After about 200 yards and just after the road bends to the right take the footpath on your left adjacent to some houses. This takes you near the river again and then across a field away from it only to meet it again where you follow it until you see the bridge under the railway on your left. Go under and up the track to the farm, through the two gates ahead and then round to your left and then right up the track again. The path goes through a gate on your left. It wasn't marked when we walked this way but on the right is a pole with an arrow on it pointing the way, so this may help you to spot the correct gate. Go through and straight across the fields ahead and you will have fun spotting the stiles. The first one isn't easy but the next one is beside a two yard stretch of stone walling in a hedge. You will see a farm ahead up on your right and your track is down the slope from this and eventually heading for the next group of buildings you can see lower down. You pass in front of these and then over a stile which leads you onto a farm track. Follow this for a few yards and then take the stile on your left which is marked as a footpath. Carry on straight ahead and then you go over a beck and bear slightly right and up through a gate and then up a short track and out onto the road. Turn left and walk into High Bentham where you can have lunch at any one of the four pubs. We had a very good bar snack at the *Coach and Horses,* which is opposite Station Road, the road up which you would have walked if you had taken the shorter route. (6.2 miles; 2 hrs 40 mins (or 4.5 miles; 1 hr 55mins))

(ℹ️) *Bentham is an old established habitation and the name is derived from the old English 'beonet-ham' meaning 'homestead where bent grass grows'. It is mentioned in the Domesday book, but only from the beginning of the fourteenth century is there documentary evidence of High and Low Bentham being separate.*

(🏃) Leaving the pub turn left and walk along the Main Street towards Low Bentham and at the *Horse and Farrier* pub turn left down Duke street and then right, at the green hut, and as the lane bends left take the stile ahead of you. With the hedge on your right go through two fields and then drop down a little to your left to go through a gate and follow the path alongside the railway. Soon you go down to your left and walk across the lines, making sure there isn't a train coming. Don't worry, this is highly unlikely since very few trains run along this line. Turn right and follow the path which follows the river.

ℹ️ *As you walk through this field you are walking through the place where the single men camped in tents at 'Bentham Holiday Camp', which took place during the summer in the first quarter of the twentieth century. The ladies and married couples were in a field across the river and the two sites were connected by a footbridge. How things change!*

🚶 You eventually pass by the fish farm referred to earlier and under the railway and out onto the road in Low Bentham. Turn left and follow the road, going first over the river and then under the railway line again. At the next junction turn left by *The Punch Bowl* up Eskew lane and soon you will glimpse Eskewbeck farm which you passed through earlier, up on the hillside ahead of you. However, you have to turn right through the woods so look out for the footpath and just below you, across the river, is Bentham Grammar School. Follow the path through the woods and as you cross the footbridge to go up the steps you walk back into Lancashire and soon you emerge out into a field.

ℹ️ *In 1726 William Collingwood left money to endow a grammar school. This was originally in High Bentham and it was only in 1948 that it moved to its present site. The school has about 300 pupils, of whom just fewer than half are boarders and is one of the oldest co-educational schools in the country. In 2002 it became the Junior section of Sedbergh School.*

🚶 Bear right but make slightly up the slope to your left and then through into the next field where you turn half left and head up the slope making for the left hand side of the right hand 'bump' of which there are two. At the crest head for the corner of the field and the gate which should be on your right ahead of you. Follow the track, right, and pass through Robert Hall farm.

ℹ️ *This farmhouse was built early in the sixteenth century on a site where a farm is reputed to have stood since Roman times. Indeed the course of the Roman road from Slaidburn to the banks of the River Wenning, just north of the farm, passes through the farm. You will notice the*

*Robert Hall, showing
unusually positioned
'garde robe' just to
one side of the front
door.*

*'garde robe' at the front of the house just up and to the left of the front
door. I do hope that when it was in use those exiting the house didn't
exit right! Don't miss the enormous chimneys which are typical of the
era in which this house was built. The house is reputed to have been
named after a fifteenth-century Roman Catholic martyr, Robert Cantsfield, who lived there.*

You pass in front of the house and then left towards a gate, but
before which you turn right and through another gate. Carry on
straight ahead and down the slope, then up the next field with
the boundary close by on your right. At the corner go over the
stile and then after about five yards turn left through the trees
then down over the beck and up into the field. Bear left and
through the next two fields heading for the farm ahead of you.
Pass by the front of the house and through the gate. Follow the
track for about 50 yards and then just past the big tree bear
diagonally left to go over a stile in the wall and then down to a

79

gate at the bottom. Follow the boundary on your right up to the house and over a stile. Turn right and then left up the track to the lane. Turn right and after about 50 yards take the footpath on your left. There may be horses in this field so straight through to the stile and then straight on again up the slope making for the big tree ahead and the house at the top. However about 25 yards past the tree turn sharp right and head for the barn on the right which you can see in the next field. You should see the stile so go over and up to the barn. On the left is a stile in the wall; go through and down to the lane. Turn right and along the lane to the old school. Here take the footpath on your left and walk up the right hand side of the field and the avenue of oak trees which is being restored. Then over the stile at the top and down and over the next stile ahead. It is quite a steep drop down now and you go over another stile and keep straight ahead making for stile which is just to the right of centre in the hedge ahead; up the next field you may be able to make out the next but one stile and the one you are seeking is dead in line with it. Go up the slope and to the stile and straight on across the next field making for the gate across. Through the gate head for the tree on the right and ahead for the stile to the right of the farm house. Turn left on the lane and then right down by the house. Head for the gate which is just to the right of the overhead wires and down to the bar. Go through the gate on your left and along the track back to your car. (5 miles; 2 hrs 10 mins)

Walk 14

Hornby to Arkholme

Outdoor Leisure Maps 41: *Forest of Bowland & Ribblesdale*
and 7 *The English Lakes SE Area*
Distance: 8 miles. Walking time: 3 hrs 30 mins
Start at Hornby car park, grid ref. SD585683
Lunch at *The Bay Horse*, 015242 21425

THIS IS A WALK which is almost entirely 'on the flat', first of all following the River Wenning and then the River Lune, though before lunch you do climb up about 45 metres (145 ft over a distance of 1 mile) on your way to the pub. The return is either downhill or on the flat since it follows the river all the way. After wet weather there can be 'damp' stretches, a common feature of riverside walks!

The car park is on the left next to the bridge on the main road, as you arrive from Lancaster.

Walk over the bridge and immediately through the gate on your left next to the first house. Follow the footpath along the River Wenning as far as you can go until it meets the Lune, where you turn right and head upstream with the river on your left. Soon you'll pass Priory Farm up on your right.

The original buildings here were constructed in the twelfth century being the 'daughter' Priory of the Premonstratensian Abbey at Croxton in Leicestershire and connected to the Abbey at Cockersand, down at the mouth of the Lune.

As you approach Loyn Bridge the path heads right and up to the road when the river is high, otherwise carry on over the stile, through the trees and under the bridge. Then climb up to your right to the gate, onto the road and over the bridge to the stile on your right.

As you walk across the bridge behind you is a small mound covered in trees. This is the site of 'Castle Stede', a Norman motte and bailey.

81

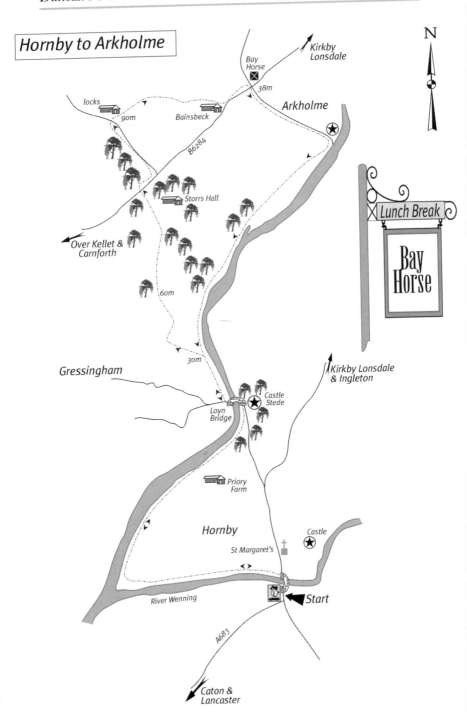

Hornby to Arkholme

Kirkby
Lonsdale

Bay
Horse

38m

Arkholme

locks

90m

Bainsbeck

B6284

Storrs Hall

Over Kellet &
Carnforth

60m

30m

Gressingham

Kirkby Lonsdale
& Ingleton

Lunch Break

Bay
Horse

Castle
Stede

Loyn
Bridge

Priory
Farm

Hornby

Castle

St Margaret's

River Wenning

Start

A683

Caton &
Lancaster

N

There is evidence that the site was earlier fortified by the Saxons or the Danes.

(🚶) Through the stile cross the field to the corner nearest the river and over the stile. Follow the path for about 150 yards and then go up the slope on your left and over a stile into the field where you follow the fence on your left. Turn right at the corner of the field and keep following the fence. Go through the gate and head diagonally right up the field to the gate which leads you into a short gathering lane for cows. Go through the gate at the other end and straight across the field, over a stile and into the field in the front of Storrs Hall. Here bear left across the field towards the trees and then through a green wooden gate out onto the road. Cross over, turn right and then left up Locka Lane to Locka Farm. Follow the footpath sign through the yard and then the gate into a short field. Cross this with the hedge on your left, go over a stile and then down the next field bearing right to the trees at the bottom. Cross over the beck and pick up the track where you bear right and, as you approach the farm, head to the left of it. There is another stile and then another which leads you out onto the road, turn left and walk up to the crossroads where you can have lunch at *The Bay Horse*. (4.8 miles; 1 hr 50 mins)

(🚶) Leaving the pub, turn left and cross the road going down the lane by the school through the village.

(ℹ) *Arkholme is an old village, originally the Norse 'Ergum', place at the shielings or hill-pastures, and as you walk down the main street you may be interested to note the names of the some of the cottages and wonder how they received these names. You will also understand why it has regularly been a strong contender in the Lancashire 'Best Kept Village' competition.*

(🚶) At the bottom of the lane take the right fork and then follow the path, keeping the fence on your right and the river away to your left.

(ℹ) *The church, constructed on the site of another motte and bailey, was formerly a chapelry of Melling so the inhabitants of the village had to cross over the Lune by ferry for weddings and funerals. At certain times this could be quite a perilous experience and it was only in 1866 that it became a parish church.*

Arkholme church, with the bailey clearly seen on the left.

🚶 At the gate/gap go through the fence and follow the trees and bushes on your left, resisting the temptation to go up and right on what seems a better path. You go over a footbridge and then the path goes in and out of trees keeping close to the river all the way back to Loyn Bridge. Here you can retrace your steps along the Lune to the confluence with the Wenning and back to Hornby. (3.8 miles; 1 hr 50 mins. If you want to take a short cut just follow the road back to the car park, in which case it will be 2.8 miles; 1 hr 20 mins)

ℹ️ *At one time Hornby was on the main thoroughfare up the Lune Valley to Scotland and consequently one of the early eighteenth-century turnpikes, so it is not surprising a castle has been on the site since the twelfth century. Raiding Scots frequently ravaged the village in what I suppose was the precursor to the present-day football and rugby matches. Today's Gothic structure, which you can see towering above the village, is reasonably modern, most of it having been built in 1848. The original castle was built just after the Conquest and was ordered to be destroyed*

Hornby Castle.

when it fell to the Roundheads but this was never carried out. There is evidence that the first building on the site was a Roman villa. The Keep was erected in the thirteenth century. St Margaret's church has an unusual octagonal tower built in 1514 by Sir Edward Stanley, Lord Monteagle the hero of Flodden Field. There are three ancient crosses which predate the Conquest, though most of the main body of the church is of nineteenth-century date.

Walk 15

Hornby to Low Bentham

Outdoor Leisure Map 41: Forest of Bowland & Ribblesdale
Distance: 10.5 miles.   Walking time: 4 hrs 10 mins
Start at Hornby car park, grid ref. SD 584683
Lunch at *The Punch Bowl*, 015242 61344

T HIS IS QUITE A LONG WALK, with very few steep
ascents, which takes you from Lancashire just into North
Yorkshire for lunch. There are some splendid views on a
good day and some parts may be a bit difficult under foot,
particularly after a spell of wet weather. About three miles
of the walk is along roads, so do take care, but at least you
can get a move on not having to watch your footing.

The car park is next to the bridge and is well marked.

Leaving the car park go over the bridge and follow the road to
the junction just past the school where you keep to the left and
follow the road to Gressingham. The road starts to go downhill
and towards Loyn bridge, so cross over to the right hand side and
go through the gap stile on your right just before the left hand
bend in the road. You are now very near to Castle Stede.

*Castle Stede is a Norman 'motte and bailey' and you will see that it
is on a very good defensive site as it overlooks what at the time was
a ford across the Lune. It would seem there is evidence of an earlier
defensive site on this spot created by the Saxons. The last defensive
creation was the pill-box you can see which was built at the start of
World War II. Would it have been effective against an advancing
German army, I ask myself!*

Carry on round the ramparts with the wall on your left and down
to the gate. Go through and then bear right towards the farm.
Here there's another gate onto the farm track and across this
there's a wooden gate on your left into a field. With the farm
track fence on your right head across the rather undulating field
in the same direction. On the hillside ahead you will see a copse

86

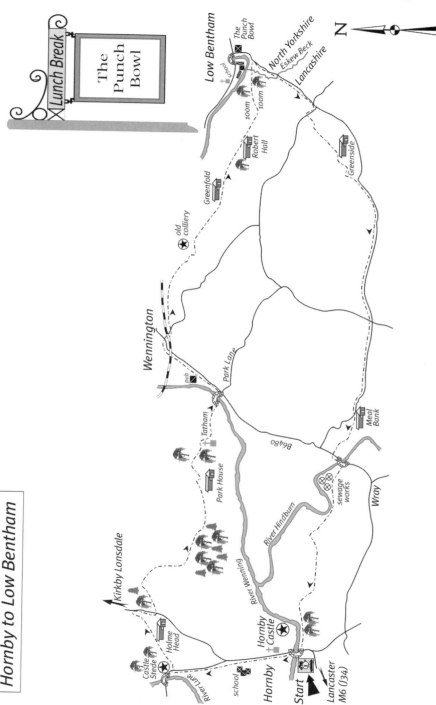

Lunch Break

The Punch Bowl

Hornby to Low Bentham

Castle Stede with the World War II 'pill box' nestling beneath it on the left.

of trees shaped rather like a whale, head to the left of this and eventually you spot a stile over onto the road. Head for this and then on the road turn right and walk up the road. This is quite a busy road so keep in single file and well to the right. After a couple of hundred yards you will see a footpath on the other side. Go over into the field and head for the tree and your left. As you get to the tree start to move to your right and up the slope so that you can follow the cart track. This takes you through a gate and you continue to follow the track until it gradually peters out. Here you continue going straight upwards with the wall about 30 metres away on your right and heading for the crown of the field. Here you can glance to your left and get a wonderful view of the Pennines and Ingleborough, on the other hand if it is a grey day you may only glimpse them through the clouds and mist. Gradually start to head right towards the wall and look out for two gates in the wall. You are going through the left hand gate. As you reach the gate turn round and see the view up the Lune Valley, towards the Howgills. As you go through the gate, bear diagonally left and soon you will see big tree sticking up across the field. This is your marker and soon you will see a ladder stile over the wall which is where you are heading. As you go over you will see a water trough 50 yards ahead by the fence. The stile next to it

*The otter waymarker
at Tatham.*

St James' Church, Tatham.

takes you into another field and on your left are some trees, leading to which is a track. Follow the track and through the short stretch of trees. There you will see another stile on your right which you go over and then follow the direction of the yellow arrow diagonally across the field. At the other side you will find a gate, so go through and into the next field where you follow the fence on your right hand side down to Park House farm. Over the hedge on your right and below is the village of Wray and Caton Moor directly behind it. Go through the gate and go straight ahead and through the yard to take the farm track on your left.

ⓘ *As the road bends right just before the church there is a big stone with an otter carved on it marking the way of the footpath going up on your left. This is quite new and the reason for it is anybody's guess. Tatham Church is dedicated to St. James and is in the Perpendicular style, with a more recent tower added in 1722. The east end stained glass windows are reputed to have come from Furness Abbey but there is no documentary evidence of this so it may well just be a good story. There has been a church on this site since 1291.*

ⓧ Follow the lane down passing over the bridge over the River Wenning and down to the main road. You may notice that the lane is marked 'Monks Gate', which may be evidence that the windows in the church are indeed from Furness Abbey. Turn left and cross over to follow the road, past *The Bridge Inn*, and as far as the newly refurbished Wennington Railway Station. This is quite a busy road so do keep in single file and taking extra care when there is a bend right hand bend ahead of you. It is best to cross over just before the pub and then cross over again when you have gone up the short rise. As you go over the next bridge you can look over to your right and see where the Lancaster–Wennington line joined up with the Skipton to Carnforth line. Soon you bear right on Old Moor road over the next railway bridge, with the station down over to your left. After about 50 yards there is a footpath on your left, so go down the track and through a gate into a field. Once in the field bear to the right and at the far side cross over a beck and over a stile, to the left of a gate. You will see a slope on your right with the vague outline of a track so follow this and go up the field with the fence and trees on your right. At the end of the field, near to the farm, you will find a gap stile in the wall. So go through and drop down to follow the path, with the wall on your left, to the barn ahead. Go through the stile next to the gate and go up the track past the farm on your left. Down on your left is a pond and the track has a line of Scots pines through which you have to pass, where the track bends to the right. There you will find a stile over the fence, with the pond right down below you on your left. Please note the stile is not marked; nor is the footpath, and it is obvious that someone intends that you will not see the stile. As you go over the stile you will see that on this side it is marked 'Public Footpath'. Turn left and follow the wall up the field. In the top corner there are a number of water board inspection chambers and a stile over the wall. This takes you onto a track. The path here goes straight ahead across the field but a simple fence has been erected which stops you doing this. You would be in your rights to cut down or push over this fence but there is a gate 20 yards to your left which you can climb over. (In fact this fence may have gone or a stile put over it when you read this.) You will see two trees sticking up across the field, so head for these, and you will find a stile over into the next field. Follow the boundary on your right and towards the farm buildings in the distance.

❶ *As you walk through this field look down to your left and through the trees you may glimpse some stone ruins, a tower structure on the left of a square structure. This is the remains of the pit head of an old colliery and it may surprise you to find that this area was at one time quite a source of coal, going back to medieval times. Most of the coal was mined using the 'bell pit' method; essentially a big but shallow pit which bulged at the bottom.*

⊛ Carry on to Green Fold farm and into the farmyard through the gate. There is a double gate to the left of the barn and through this you cross the field heading for a spot halfway between the big tree in the bottom right hand corner and the gate. There you will find a stile into the next field where you carry on bearing slightly to the right and heading for the trees where you will find a stile. Then over the beck and up the steps to your left which take you through some bushes and trees. After about 30 yards you will see a stile up on your right which takes you into another field. Go down to the stile at the bottom and then up towards the farm house ahead.

St James' Church, Tatham, showing the east end window.

ℹ️ *As you approach the house you will notice the vast chimney structure and this tells you that the building is of the early sixteenth century. It is called 'Robert Hall' and named after Robert Cantsfield, a Catholic martyr. It was built about 1512 and part of it was a secret Catholic chapel. There is evidence that there has been a farm building here for many centuries prior to this building and it is built on the course of the Roman road which came over the fells from Slaidburn.*

🚶 Carry on past the house and the twentieth-century farm buildings and follow the track. After about five minutes there is a gate into a field on your left. This isn't marked as a footpath but it is and as you enter the field follow the vague track and go between the two crowns and down the field bearing slightly right. You will see a boundary and in the corner is a beck which you go over and head for the trees keeping right and below the slope. You will come across two stiles, so go over the right hand one and down the steps through the trees to a footbridge. You will see Bentham Grammar School across the river.

❶ *As you go over the footbridge you are crossing not only Eskew Beck but also the boundary between Lancashire and North Yorkshire. This is an ancient boundary going back through the ages but in more recent times, times when things were written down, it was the boundary of 'Burton Chase' which, from the immediate post-Domesday period, was held by the Mowbray family who held all the hunting rights by gift of the king. The circumference of the chase was about 64 miles and included Gregareth, Ingleborough and Pen-y-ghent.*

(🏃) Follow the track up through the trees and out onto the road. Here you turn left and downhill to Low Bentham. In a minute or two you will be at a junction and there is *The Punch Bowl*, where you stop for lunch. (6 miles; 2 hrs 15 mins)

❶ *Of the two Benthams, High and Low, the village you are now in is believed to be the more ancient, though there is little documentary evidence to support that claim. It is known that a Roman road from Ribchester passed very close to the west end of the present habitation and the church is of Saxon foundation. High Bentham doesn't have any claims as valid as these. The name is of old English derivation; originally called 'beonet − ham', homestead near the bent grass. The grammar school was endowed in 1726 and was originally in High Bentham, moving to its present site in 1948. It is one of the longest established co-educational boarding schools in the country.*

(🏃) Leaving the pub retrace your steps up the lane but continue on up where you entered it from the trees earlier. After about 500 yards you go over a bridge by the entrance to Eskewbeck farm and Eskew beck flowing beneath it is the same beck you crossed over into Yorkshire earlier. So you are now back into Lancashire. Carry on up the road for another 500 yards until you turn right into Old Moor road, which you entered earlier at Wennington station. Over in the distance is Ingleborough and Whernside further to the right. Looking to the left of Ingleborough is Gregareth which is the highest spot in present-day Lancashire. Soon you will be at Hunter's Barn where you turn left and go through the gate as the track bends to the right. Bear diagonally right across the field, eventually you will see a farmhouse down below you, Greenside, which you head for. Before you get there you have to pass through a broken down wall and across some rather boggy ground. Pass round to the right of the farm and through a gate

onto a track. As a matter of fact the public footpath passes round
the other side of the farm and in to the farmyard but the other
way is easiest and obviously the route which the farmer would
prefer you to take. As the track bends round to the left go straight
ahead and then to your right through a gate where you turn left
and go up the field heading for the house you can see on the
skyline. At the top is a stile out onto the road. Turn right and
follow this road, keeping in single file on the right hand side. You
follow this road for one mile down to the crossroads and then
straight ahead up the intriguingly named Trinket lane as far as
Meal Bank farm on your left, about 800 yards from the crossroads.
Turn left into the yard then right through two gates, the way is
marked by yellow arrows so you will not be in doubt. In the field
there is the remains of a boundary, signified by a hump along the
field. Keep to the left of this and at the trees the path drops sharply
down to a stile out onto the road. Turn left and cross over the
road and as you cross the bridge take the path to your right along
a bridleway. This brings you out at a sewage farm, where you
bear left and then over a rather indistinct stile into a field. Go
across to the right hand corner and over another indistinct stile
where you have to negotiate a barbed wire fence before you turn
right to follow the path round the edge of the field with the River
Hindburn down to your right. You will find the path clearly
marked now and you go to the left through five fields going over
the stiles from one to the other. In the sixth field you are nearing
Hornby and here you bear right towards the river, not going
ahead towards the mound covered with trees. The path emerges
onto a farm track where you bear left and follow it out onto the
main road through Hornby. Here you cross over and to your car.
(4.5 miles; 1 hr 55 mins)

Walk 16

Leighton Moss to Arnside

Outdoor Leisure Map 7:   The English Lakes SE Area
Distance: 9.6 miles.   Walking time: 4 hrs 35 mins
Start at Leighton Moss RSPB visitor centre car park,
grid ref. SD477750
Lunch at *The Albion* (01524 761226)
or *Ye Olde Fighting Cocks* (01524 761203)

YOU WILL DEFINITELY MEET OTHER PEOPLE on this walk whenever you do it but it is still an interesting walk. Starting by the bird sanctuary you climb up over the golf course and through woods to Silverdale, then along the coast on a good path to Arnside and *The Albion* for lunch. The return is over Arnside Knot (159 metres) and Eaves Wood.

Go back to the entrance to the centre and turn left onto the road over the railway bridge and right at the junction, towards the old railway station. Just pass this take a left hand turning over the stile onto the golf course. Walk up the slope following the obvious path and at the crest you will notice in front of you a few white marker sticks across the golf course which you follow, taking care not to interfere with those who are 'spoiling a good walk'! You are gradually rising up as you cross over the course and as you approach the wall you will notice a telephone pole, head towards this and go through the gap stile in the wall and turn right up the lane. After about 50 yards follow the footpath sign to the left, just before a bungalow, and follow the path through the woods and down to a stile. You will now be in Lambert's meadow, which you cross and then go over a footbridge and through a gap stile in the wall. Turn left and follow the track until it comes out on the road and turn left. At the junction turn right towards the centre of the village of Silverdale. Where the road bends right, towards the centre, carry straight on along Shore Road. After about 150 yards you will come to some steps up on your right,

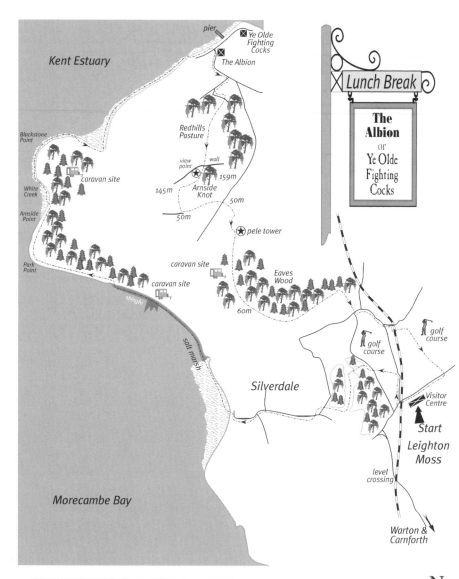

Leighton Moss to Arnside

N

Looking west across New Barns bay towards Blackstone Point.

opposite the retirement home, these lead into a field which you cross following the obvious route. At the end of the field you go through a swing gate and carry on down to the right hand corner of the field and through another gate. The path leads down to the cove where you go through another gate and left and then right along the shore.

❶ *If it is a spring tide with a stiff westerly breeze you won't be able to do this so alternatively you'll have to take the lane up from the cove and then left along the road eventually taking the first left into a caravan site.*

🚶 Walk along the beach under the cliffs right as far as you can go, then clamber up over the rocks onto the path through the woods which you follow round past Park Point and Arnside Point. Do take care whilst on this path, in places it comes quite close to the edge and there is a steep drop down. Eventually you will see a cove below you, so drop down and you're at White Creek. If the tide is out you can nip straight across to Blackstone Point or otherwise follow the high tide mark round on the rocks. Carry on round scrambling over the rather uneven rocks until you come out at New Barns bay. Again you can cut the corner if the tide's out, though it is not to be recommended since the sand and mud can be somewhat of a hazard. It is easier to walk round to the bridge on the track and turn left at the trees. Follow this path along the shore to Arnside, eventually emerging on the promenade where you can have a bar meal at *The Albion*, or *Ye Olde Fighting*

Cocks, just a bit further on. (5.4 miles; 2 hrs 15 mins)

❶ *If you are lucky enough to be walking along the shore at high tide, especially a neap tide, you will enjoy the view of the bore coming up the Kent estuary. Under certain conditions this can be quite spectacular as the incoming tide rushes up the Kent estuary. This is preceded by blasts on a hooter which is to warn those on the sands to seek the refuge of dry land so as not to be caught up in the oncoming flood!*

🚶 Turn left out of the pub and follow Silverdale road uphill. At the top turn right up Redhills Road in the direction of Arnside Knott. After 100 yards turn left up High Knott road turning left at the top and past the rather splendid houses on your right. After about 150 yards take the footpath on your right up through the trees and over the ladder stile into a field, this is Upper Redhills pasture. Look up for the highest point in the field and head for that; the path is discerned by noting a darker shade of green in the grass.

❶ *This is always the easiest way to spot a path through a field; the pressure of many feet on the earth compresses the soil so that when it rains the soil holds the water and the grass grows stronger and greener. For a few years early in the twentieth century this was a nine-hole golf course. The pasture has gained its name from the red colour of the soil and during the eighteenth century iron ore was extracted from here and transported to Leighton Beck were there was a blast furnace.*

🚶 The path leads up to a gate through the wall so turn right to the lookout with a bench where you can rest awhile and enjoy the view over to the Lakeland Fells.

❶ *Behind you and up a bit through the trees is the trig point at the top of the Knot. Below you are larch trees remaining from those planted in 1841. Most of these were cut down during the First World War.*

🚶 Having taken in the view carry on following the path and at the first junction, by another bench, turn left downhill and through some more trees and eventually through a gate and to another path where you turn left at the junction. Go down this path to the road, but take care and look right for passing traffic! Across the road take the lane down towards Arnside Tower before which you pass through a farm yard.

❶ *Sadly the pele tower is in a bad state of repair but once would have* *been a magnificent example of a fortified tower built in the fourteenth century to provide refuge for the farmer and his stock when the marauding Scots arrived.*

🏃 Carry on up and over a ladder stile. Head up the path opposite following the sign to Silverdale and Eaves Wood. Eventually you come across the road through the caravan site bear right just a bit and at the junction bear left up the grassy bank next to the play area. Once up the bank bear right and then left up through the trees with caravans on your right. At the wall go through the gap and then carry on down to another wall and gap stile onto a lane with some houses on your right. Not far along is a bench where you bear left up the path to Eaves Wood and Waterslack.

ℹ️ *Eaves Wood contains a large proportion of ancient and semi-natural woodland as well as a great variety of deciduous trees. In the trees there is also a good variety of birdlife, perhaps the most interesting being the elusive hawfinch which is one of the most secretive and quiet natured birds to be found high in the treetops. It is more easy to see in winter when they have a tendency to form flocks.*

🏃 After about half a mile there is a footpath signpost and here you turn right following the white concessionary arrow down a path to the road; on your right will be a Guide Camp with a wooden hut in the field. At the road turn left and, ignoring the first turn on your right, turn right at the T junction and walk along the road to Leighton Moss. After about 300 yards there is a cul-de-sac on your left so go down this and then take the footpath on your right by the houses. Just along the wall on your left is a ladder stile which leads you down onto the railway line. Take care when crossing, there is a bend just up to your right so you can't see trains coming – but hopefully you'll hear them if there are any. Go over the wall on the other side and follow the track to your right; this bends round left and uphill a bit past old buildings on your left which are much overgrown. At the junction turn right and through a gate back onto the golf course. Cross this, again taking care of those playing the royal and ancient game, bearing left a bit for the stile in the wall opposite. Then go diagonally left across the hummocky field and through the stile onto the road, where you turn right back to the visitor centre car park. (4.2 miles; 2 hrs 20 mins)

Walk 17

Littledale, Roeburndale Road, to Wray

Outdoor Leisure Map 41:   Forest of Bowland & Ribblesdale
Distance: 9.7 miles.   Walking time: 4 hrs 5 mins
Start at the road gate at Winder, grid ref. SD 592628
Lunch at *The George and Dragon*, 015242 21403

THE START OF THIS WALK is undulating for the first 3 miles and then gradually drops down through fields and along tracks and then the road to the delightful village of Wray. The return is much shorter and involves a return uphill on the road the way you came. The route then gradually leads you back uphill to your car and with just an occasional drop down the return is all up hill. During and after wet weather some stretches are particularly boggy!

🚶 Leave your car in a convenient place near to the gate marked with the sign 'Public Road' and go through the gate, or over the grid, and down the road to the next gate on your right and where the left hand turn is marked with a 'no entry' sign. Go through the gate and down the lane and then up again to Haylot Farm. Turn sharply left through the gate and follow this track down and you will be able to look to your left and see where you've come from. The track eventually crosses a bridge over the River Roeburn and then climbs up again. After about 150 yards you will see a footpath going up to your right, where the corner of a wall turns away from the road side. Go over the stile and follow the wall up the meadow. At the top you come to a stile over onto a lane, cross over and go over the opposite stile into another field. Bear slightly right and up and to the corner of the field. Then go through to the next field, which is rather rough, and head for the far corner on your right looking for a stile. Over this you follow the wall on your right hand side and in the next field carry on in the same direction but bearing just slightly left and more or less contouring till you come across another path where you bear left and drop down to the footbridge over the beck by the waterfall. Go up to

100

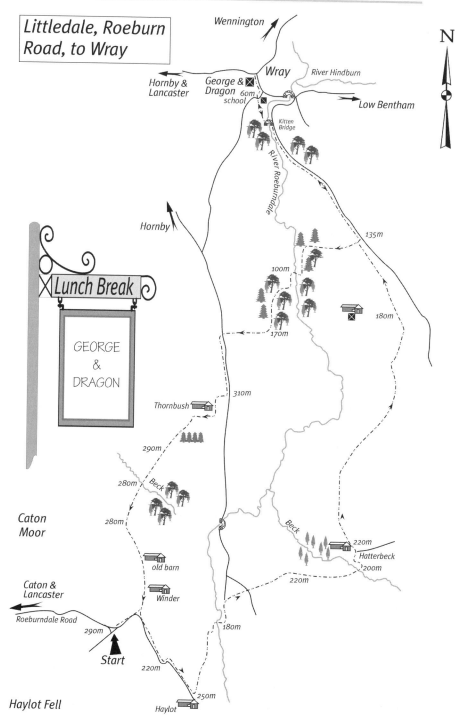

Littledale, Roeburn
Road, to Wray

Wennington

Wray

River Hindburn

Hornby &
Lancaster

George &
Dragon   school

6om

Low Bentham

Kitten
Bridge

River Roeburndale

N

Hornby

135m

Lunch Break

100m

GEORGE
&
DRAGON

170m

180m

310m

Thornbush

290m

Beck

280m

Caton
Moor

280m

Beck

220m

Hatterbeck

old barn

200m

Caton &
Lancaster

Winder

220m

Roeburndale Road

290m

180m

Start

220m

Haylot Fell

250m

Haylot

Wray Endowed School, showing Captain Pooley's memorial over the door and the circular Bryan Holme blue plaque on the left.

a track and left through the ford and to the farmyard where you turn right and then immediately left over a stile. Right through the first gate and along the fence on your right and then over the stile in the wall onto a track which you follow right and down to the bottom of the field and pass by the barn with it on your right. You then quite simply follow the path through numerous fields keeping the boundary on your right, and onto rough land at Wray Wood Moor; the old quarry is down on your right.

There is also evidence of 'bell-pit' mines where coal was taken by digging down through the earth and into a pit which widened at the bottom almost in the shape of a bell, hence its name.

You then go through a gate onto a green lane and then out into a field which leads you to the farm track. Here you go over a stile in the wall and carry straight on with the remains of an old wall on your left. In the third field bear right to the stile onto the road and turn left downhill. After about a mile and just through Kitten Bridge, take the path left, known as 'The Spout' which leads you past Wray Endowed school and into Wray.

ℹ️ *The endowment was made by Captain Richard Pooley who died in 1684. He left '£200 for ever' and a Board of Trustees still administers the fund which has grown out of the original sum, which seems small, but was equivalent to about 20 men's annual wages at the time. Richard Pooley's story is a fascinating one but sadly too long to tell here. If you are interested no doubt someone in the village will be able to tell you about him. Almost a hundred years after the school was opened a young pupil started at the school named, Bryan Holme. Later he started a legal career in Lancaster and later played an important role in his profession by founding the Law Society, the controlling body of lawyers in this country. Wray was devastated by a flood in August 1967 and this swept away many of the houses near to the River Roeburn. The village has many fascinating nooks and crannies and is well worth visiting during the period of the May Bank Holiday when, at the time of writing, a Scarecrow Festival is held lasting about a week. Many households throughout the village create thematic 'scarecrows' with which they adorn their dwellings.*

🚶 Turn left into the main street and walk though the village. Near to the junction is *The George and Dragon.* (5.4 miles; 2 hrs 10 mins) Just round the corner to the left and on the main road you will also find *The New Inn.*

🚶 Having had lunch retrace your steps back to Kitten Bridge and up the road to the place where you emerged out onto the road earlier. In this field carry straight on, not turning left uphill the way you came. You go over a stile and down with a wall on your left. In the next field your bear slightly right, basically going down the middle of the field and in the next field you carry on down to the trees and look for a stile into the woods. It is not easy to find, or wasn't the last time we passed this way, but it is nearer to the right hand bottom corner of the field than the left hand corner. Follow the path down through the trees and it bends left and eventually you are at the bottom of the woods; the path eventually becoming a track as it approaches a footbridge. Cross over and go to your left following a track up which bends to the right and then to the left and then right again but before this you take the left spur, the path rising gradually up the side of a slope. You may be able to glimpse a windmill up on your right and also become aware of a lot of woodcraft people, or at least evidence of them. Carry on up and through the trees then follow the path up with a wall on your right. You then follow the track in a curve towards the farmhouse and there you turn sharp right to follow the track out onto Moor Lane. Turn left, uphill, and follow the road for about 400 yards and then turn right following the footpath sign to Thornbush and Winder and where the signpost says '1¼ miles to Winder, 2 miles to Deep Clough'. Go up the track and through the farmyard and then right, straight up the field to the hedge and then left up to the line of trees and over the stile. Carry straight on up with the fence on your right and then into the next field where you go over the crest and straight down to the wall where with luck you will find the steps over the wall. These will probably be to your left down the slope and is just to the right of the trees you can see on the sides of Warm Beck Gill. Go over the step stile and down to the beck and up and then bearing slightly left head up the rough field to the gate on the track. Go through this and then follow the track past Hill Barn to Winder and back to your car. (4.3 miles; 1 hr 55 mins)

Walk 18

Middleton to Sunderland Point

Explorer Map 41:   *Lancaster, Morecambe & Fleetwood*

Distance: 5.3 miles.   Walking time: 2 hrs 15 mins

Start at Carr lane, grid ref. SD 423587

BEFORE SETTING OFF ON YOUR WALK IT IS WORTH FINDING OUT
WHEN IT IS HIGH TIDE. THE ROUTE FROM SUNDERLAND POINT TO
OVERTON IS CUT OFF BY WATER FOR ABOUT TWO HOURS EVERY
HIGH TIDE.

Lunch at *The Globe Inn*, 01524 858224

A VERY SHORT WALK suitable for a winter's day when the daylight hours are few, but also a delightful walk in midsummer, spring or autumn when the estuary birds are around. It also includes a visit to Sambo's grave. The road to Sunderland Point is cut off for about three hours at high tide so check up before you start, though the outward route as detailed gives access at all times. Therefore lunch is arranged at Overton with just a short walk home afterwards.

Park your car in a suitable place in Middleton: Carr Lane, the road to the old holiday camp, is the most suitable, and head down the lane with the 'footpath' sign on it and take the right fork towards the coast. After passing through about five fields the path brings you out onto Carr Lane again. Turn left and soon the lane ends at Potts Corner and here you simply follow the coastline south to Sunderland Point. It is a bit rough underfoot and you're walking on sand and pebbles.

About 500 yards before you get to the Point look out for Sambo's grave which is in a little plot on your left, just after the path which leads across to the dwellings on the eastern shore of the Point. A lot of myth surrounds Sambo who was reputedly a black African slave who was rescued by a ship's master and acted as his attendant. We certainly know he died in 1736 and it is said that he was left at the Ship Inn while his master went away on business. Sambo thought he was deserted, fell ill, refused all food and therefore died. It was probably fever.

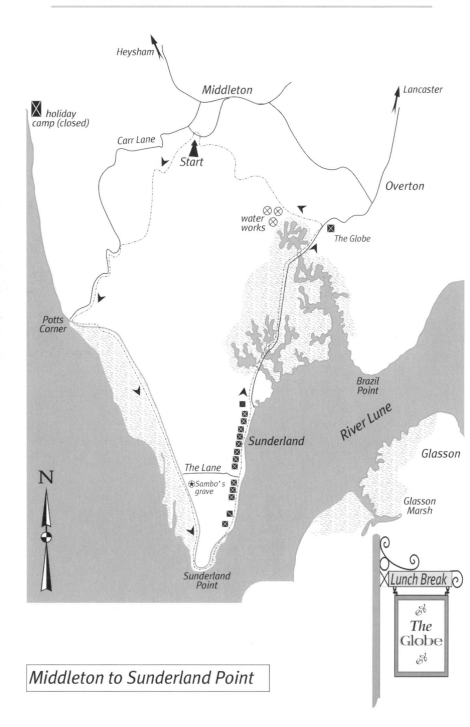

Middleton to Sunderland Point

The hamlet of Sunderland Point, looking south to the estuary of the River Lune.

Here lies

Poor SAMBO

A faithfull NEGRO

Who (attending his Master from the West Indies)

DIED on his arrival at SUNDERLAND

Full sixty Years the angry Winter's Wave

Has thundering dashd this bleak & barren shore

Since SAMBO'S Head laid in this lonely GRAVE

Lies still & ne'er will hear their turmoil more.

Full many a Sand bird chirps upon the Sod

And many a Moonlight Elfin round him trips

Full many a Summer's Sunbeam warms the Clod

And many a teeming Cloud upon him drips

But still he sleeps – till the awakening Sounds

Of the Archangel's Trump new Life impart

Then the GREAT JUDGE his approbation founds

Not on Man's COLOR but his WORTH of HEART

❶ *The 'Epitaph to Sambo' to be found on a plaque beside Sambo's grave at Sunderland Point. Written in 1796, 60 years after Sambo's death, by the Rev. James Watson*

🚶 Follow the coast round the Point and eventually you will arrive onto a coastal path which leads you into the hamlet of Sunderland.

❶ *Prior to the opening of St George's Quay in Lancaster and then the opening of Glasson Dock this was a busy port, though it is hard to believe that now. It is said that the first cotton to be imported commercially for manufacture in England was brought into Sunderland Point. This may be the reason that an unusual tree which overhung the path until 1998 was known as the 'cotton tree'. It is believed that it started to grow just after cotton started to arrive and, since no one knew what sort of tree it was, logical thought assumed it to be a cotton tree. You won't be surprised to learn there are a number of stories or myths about Sunderland Point and this is just one of them!*

🚶 Walk along the 'promenade' and you eventually find yourself on a proper road which traverses Lades Marsh, where you may be lucky enough to spot a great variety of birds attracted by the rich pickings of the flats. After just over a mile you arrive on the fringes of Overton and you will find *The Globe Inn* on your right. (4.6 miles; 1 hr 55 mins)

🚶 Leaving the pub turn left and then first right down the lane and after about 300 yards, where the lane bends round to the left, take the right turn past the water board workings and follow the path back across five fields to Middleton and your car. (0.8 miles; 20 mins)

Walk 19

Over Kellet to Burton-in-Kendal

Outdoor Leisure Map 7: The English Lakes SE area
Distance: 10.8 miles. Walking time: 4 hrs 20 mins
Start at the Green, grid ref. SD 524700
Lunch at *The King's Arms*, 01524 781409

THIS WALK is mainly across field paths to Burton and then returns along lanes and the Lancaster Canal towpath, with just short stretches across fields. If you do this in the spring, when the grass can be long in some pastures, the return will be much easier than the outward journey. On a good day you will have wonderful views towards the Lakes and after wet weather some of the going will be muddy.

❶ *Referred to as Chellet in the Domesday Book and of Norse derivation meaning a 'slope with a spring', Kellet Seeds (130 m.) is the highest point near to the village though this is now almost in the centre of the quarry, Nether Kellet being lower down the slope. The spring's whereabouts is a matter of conjecture.*

🏃 Park your car beside a small green next to the Old Wesleyan Chapel on the road through Over Kellet going in the direction of Kirkby Lonsdale, or in any convenient and unobtrusive place. The green is about 200 yards past the crossroads in the centre of the village. Having parked your car cross over the road and go down the passage leading to a chicken farm. It is opposite a white cottage which overlooks the green and with 'E I T 1854' over the door. Go over the cattle grid and past the broiler houses. Soon there is a gate on your left so go through and follow the hedge on your right. Go over two stiles and then you carry on with the slope up on your right. There will be some trees ahead, so go towards these and you will see a stile into the trees. Go over and soon you will pass through the trees and be in a field where you bear left and the slope of the field will be down to your right as you approach a gate in the fence. Through this bear slightly right and down

Over Kellet to Burton-in-Kendal

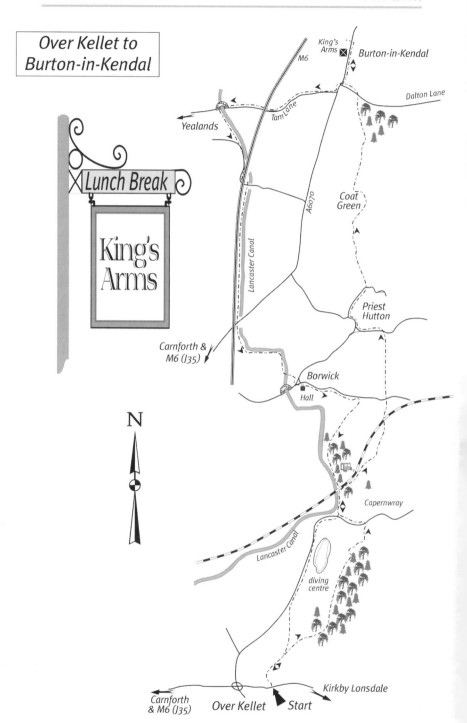

King's Arms

Burton-in-Kendal

M6

King's Arms

Dalton Lane

Yealands

Tarn Lane

Coat Green

A6070

Lancaster Canal

Priest Hutton

Carnforth & M6 (J35)

Borwick

Hall

N

Capernwray

Lancaster Canal

diving centre

Carnforth & M6 (J35)

Over Kellet

Start

Kirkby Lonsdale

Lunch Break

King's Arms

where you will find a stile by the corner of the trees. Go over and turn left to follow the track down to the road. Turn left again and at Capernwray Old Hall you turn right down a lane soon following a sign pointing to New England. This is a private road but a public right of way so don't hesitate to go along it and onto the canal towpath.

There's been a hall here since the beginning of the thirteenth century, the name deriving from the Norse for 'merchant's corner'. As you walk on the towpath you go over the Keer Aqueduct and across the canal on the parapet is a notice informing you that, 'Keer Aqueduct 43 ft long 35 ft high and first used in 1797'.

Just before the railway bridge turn right and follow the track and with the embankment up on your left. Eventually the path bears right, away from the railway line, and you follow the path through three fields. There is a stile in the bottom right hand corner of

The canal basin at Tewitfield. Once a hive of activity and now a restful backwater.

the first and then you keep the boundary on your right to go over another stile over which you bear left and head across the field, with the slope up on your left, back towards the railway line and a bridge going under it. Follow the right hand track up to the road. Cross over and the path goes through a farmyard and then three fields. In the second field the path follows a farm track and eventually you emerge out onto a lane where you turn left and follow the road into Priest Hutton. Keep bearing right at the junctions and soon you will be following a narrow lane with houses and bungalows on your left. The sealed road ends and you take the left hand fork following the track for about 300 yards. Then you cross a field to go over the stile ahead where you keep right and follow the path, and across the county boundary into Cumbria, before the path circles round to left with a farm on your left. Just past the farm take the path on your right, which again is up a track. Carry straight on at the top with the slope of a small wooded hill up on your left and then at the next fork in the path take the left hand one which eventually brings you out onto a road on the outskirts of Burton-in-Kendal. Turn left and then right to follow the road into Burton where you will find *The Kings Arms.* (5 miles; 2 hrs)

(✦) After lunch turn right out of the pub and retrace your steps back out of the village and take the right hand turning into Tarn Lane, not the left hand one from where you entered the village. Follow the road for almost a mile, crossing over the M6, until you arrive at the canal bridge. Cross over and go down to the towpath where you turn right, or south, and follow the canal until where take the track out onto the road and turn right. This takes you over the M6 and just over it there is a path on your right which brings you back onto the towpath again.

(ℹ) *At this point you may well ponder upon the actions of those bureaucrats; officers, councillors and Government ministers, who in the late 1960s decided not to build adequate bridges under the M6 in order to save what in fact was a miserable sum of money. This effectively closed the canal for its last ten miles between Tewitfield and Kendal. May they be remembered as blinkered fools, and wouldn't it be fitting if suitable memorials could be erected on each of the bridges in memory of their misguided decision! The good news is that at the time of writing (early 2000), positive moves are being made to right the wrong and hopefully this stretch will be open again to link Kendal and the Lake District to the rest of the canals of England and Wales via the new link being built west of Preston to the Leeds & Liverpool Canal via the River Ribble and the River Douglas.*

(🚶) Continue alongside the remnants of the canal, passing the redundant locks, until you reach Tewitfield and the northern extremity of the Lancaster Canal where you will find a number of boats tied up. At the second bridge go up to the track and turn left over the bridge to follow it out to the village of Borwick.

(ℹ) *Here is Borwick Hall, now a youth training centre run by Lancashire County Council. There has been a hall here since a mansion house was created around a medieval pele tower which is thought to have been built by Thomas Whittington. Its most famous owner was Sir Robert Bindloss who was at one time MP for Lancaster. He was a determined persecutor of Quakers and was County Sheriff from 1671 to 1673.*

(🚶) As you emerge into the village keep to the left, but don't turn sharp left, taking the road which goes past the entry to Borwick Hall and is signposted to Kirkby Lonsdale. Follow this road for about half a mile and as it goes downhill you will find a footpath over a ladder stile on your right. Go down the field with the hedge on your right and then over the stile at the bottom, then another one through the narrow passage. Over the next stile bear right diagonally across the field and then over another stile to head up the field towards the caravans. You will find a stile over which is a notice advising you that you are in private property. Well you may be, but it is a public right of way. Turn right and follow the footpath down through the trees and soon you come to the side of a canal basin.

(ℹ) *There used to be a limestone quarry where some of the caravans now stand and this basin was where canal boats would come and collect the stone. It was served by an overhead tramway.*

(🚶) Follow the path and soon you are alongside the canal proper again but on the opposite side to that you were on earlier. Leave the caravan site and follow the track back under the railway line and out onto the road. Turn right here and follow the road for just over half a mile where you will find a stile over into a field on your left. This may be obscured by the foliage so don't miss it. It is a double stile and once over it bear right to the stile in the next hedge, go up the next field bearing right still and at the top go over the next stile on your right. There is another stile opposite and then you bear diagonally left to the corner of the field. You will now find yourself on a path you were on at the start of the walk. Follow it back to Over Kellet and your car. (5.8 miles; 2 hrs 20 mins)

Walk 20

Over Kellet to Yealand Conyers

Outdoor Leisure Map 7: The English Lakes SE Area
Distance: 9.8 miles.   Walking time: 4 hrs 20 mins
Start at The Green Square next to the Old Wesleyan Chapel,
grid ref. SD524700
Lunch at *The New Inn*, 01524 732938

HEADING NORTH over the fields, you walk along the
Lancaster Canal a bit before taking to the fields again
then north along the first bit of closed canal alongside the
M6 before eventually crossing under it for lunch at *The New
Inn*. The return takes you through an interesting wood before crossing the M6, again by tunnel, before once more
returning through the fields.

Park your car next to the Old Wesleyan Chapel and the green
bounded by big rocks.

ⓘ *The village was mentioned as 'Chellet' in the Domesday Book, which
is from the Norse and means 'slope with a spring'. The village is
certainly on the slope of the hill which is now being gradually taken
away as it is 'Leapers Wood Quarry'. The exact place where the spring
is to be found is a mystery.*

⚐ Head down the footpath on the opposite side of the road from the
white cottage with the letters E I T 1854 painted in black over
the door. Go between the houses and over the cattle grid and
down past the broiler houses. Carry on and you will find a gate
to your left, go through this then follow the fence on your right,
over one stile and then another and follow the contour line round
with the slope on your right until you come to the trees. Whilst
contouring round you will be just below a natural fault in the
land. Go over the stile into the trees and straight up and out into
a field. You should pick up a path bearing left which you follow
going upwards and to a gate where you turn slightly right heading
for the next stile in the corner of the field down by the trees. You

Over Kellet to Yealand Conyers

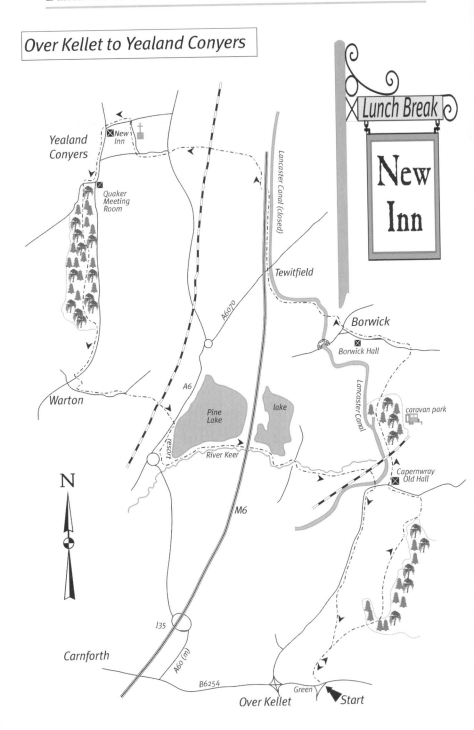

Lunch Break

New Inn

Yealand Conyers

New Inn

Quaker Meeting Room

Lancaster Canal (closed)

Tewitfield

Borwick

Borwick Hall

A6070

Lancaster Canal

caravan park

Warton

A6

Pine Lake

lake

resort

River Keer

Capernwray Old Hall

N

M6

J35

Carnforth

A60 (m)

B6254

Over Kellet

Green

Start

then go over another stile out onto the road to the caravan site where you turn left down to the main road. Turn left here and at Capernwray Old Hall, after 300 yards, turn right following the sign to New England! Don't go over the bridge but bear right and follow the track where a notice informs you, 'Private Road cul-de-sac New England only' – it is still a public right of way for those on foot. Soon you're on the canal towpath which goes under the railway bridge and into the caravan park. Go sharp left here keeping to the canal bank and soon you turn away from the canal into a quiet backwater which you walk along then carry on up through the trees. At the top you will see a stile on your left, just before you get to more caravans and the 'Private' sign. Go over into the field and head down and to your right and in the very bottom right hand corner you enter into a narrow spur of land at the end of which is a stile through the wall. There is then another similar stile into a field then keep the fence on your left and walk up to another stile in a wall onto the road. Turn left and into Borwick.

ⓘ *Borwick Hall, on your left as you enter the village, is now a residential conference and training centre. The beautiful Elizabethan house was mainly created by the Bindloss family who were wealthy Kendal merchants. A pele tower constitutes part of the hall and this was built in 1499 by Thomas Whittington. The future Charles II stayed at Borwick shortly before his defeat in battle at Worcester and when he subsequently acquired the throne Sir Robert Bindloss was installed as Knight of the Shire and was County Sheriff in 1671–73. Sir Robert was a persecutor of Quakers and died without a male heir in 1688 when the estate passed into the hands of the Towneleys and later to the Stricklands of Sizergh. Like many old houses this one is reputed to be haunted.*

⊛ At the Green turn right and then turn left between some houses following the indistinct footpath signpost. This takes you down a short lane to the canal bridge where you go down to your right and onto the towpath. Turn left and along the towpath till the canal's unfortunate termination at Tewitfield. You then take the path round to the left under the road, alongside the motorway, and then carry on following the old towpath alongside the remains of the former canal.

ⓘ *As you walk alongside the remains of the canal you may wish to wonder*

The canal basin at Tewitfield.

at the folly of those who made the decision to cut off the northern reaches due to the construction of the M6. It is understood that by doing so £10,000 per bridge was saved! It wouldn't happen today, that's for sure. What a pity that canal boats cannot sail north into Kendal. It would surely be one of the most popular stretches of canal in the country. The good news, as this is being written, is that there is a plan to revive the canal right through to Kendal; the estimated cost being £25 million!

As you continue along the towpath you pass four old locks, now just weirs, and at the first bridge turn left onto a track down and under the motorway. Follow the track up and then go left over a stile and follow the fence on your right until you come onto a track over the railway line and down to the road (A6). Cross over and up the lane opposite and take the first right hand junction down the lane past the church and at the next junction turn left up to the New Inn at Yealand Conyers. (5 miles; 2 hrs 5 mins)

As a matter of interest to those who like to pronounce places as do the locals, it is known as 'Yelland Conyers' and so are the other Yealands in the area. The adjoining village is Yealand Redmayne and the two are so called since according to the 'Testa de Nevill' Matthew de Redman and Robert de Kymyers both held an eighth part of a knight's fee (or fiefdom) in Yealand, which clearly shows the origin of the addition to the term Yealand.

🚶 Turn left out of the pub and up hill through the village, a good start after lunch, and at the top turn right into Peter Lane.

ℹ️ *Just before you turn right on your left hand side is the Quaker Meeting House built in 1697. Just under the eaves is a clock placed in what was formerly a circular window. It is in memory of Richard Hubberthorne, a local man and a martyr who met his death in London in 1662. This part of Lancashire was a strong base of 'The Society of Friends', the original Quakers and whose members were often successful in trade and in turn great benefactors; as indeed they still are.*

🚶 Carry on up the road and round the left hand bend for about 200 yards, then take the path signposted on your left through Hyning woods. You soon come into a field and across this is a little white gate in a wall into more woods. Follow the track through these making sure you don't drop down to your left but going straight down through the trees for about half a mile, at the end turning

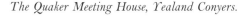

The Quaker Meeting House, Yealand Conyers.

right. Then you go over a stile onto a track where you turn left and eventually out onto the road, turning right into Warton. After you enter the village and about 200 yards on your left you will see a track guarded by metal barriers. Go down here and then right eventually coming out onto the road near the Methodist church. Turn left and follow the road till it bears left a bit near an enormous barn on the right. Take the track to your right, down under the railway bridge and on to the main road (A6). Go straight across and follow the path to the right alongside Pine Lake resort. At the entrance to the resort cross over and go to the left, inside the fence, and follow this round to the beck where you turn left and follow it all the way to the bridge under the motorway. Carry on following the beck until you come out onto the road at Keer bridge. Cross over the bridge and then down through the gate on your left following the beck on its opposite bank. As you approach the railway arches go under the nearest, or right hand one, and up the field to the gate in the top left hand corner. Then follow the track over the canal and onto the road at Capernwray Hall. Turn right and follow the road towards Over Kellet. Go past the quarry and then after about another 600 yards take the path on your left by going through the hedge over a double stile and directly across the field to the stile opposite. Cross the footbridge and then bearing slightly right go across and up the field. Over the stile and across this field to the stile half way along the hedge and then across the next field to the gate in the top right hand corner. Then follow the path back past the broiler houses to your car. (4.8 miles; 2 hrs 15 mins)

Walk 21

Silverdale to Arnside

Outdoor Leisure Map 7:   The English Lakes SE Area

Distance: 8.0 miles.   Walking time: 3 hrs 15 min

Start at Shore Road on the slip road to the beach,
grid ref. SD 458748

Lunch at *The Albion* (01524 761226)
or *Ye Old Fighting Cocks* (01524 761203)

ONE OF THE FAVOURITE WALKS for those living in
North-West England; also probably the most well-
trodden walk in the book. The attractions, apart from the
unique geology and rare species, vary including: a walk along
the beach, followed by a cliff top walk and then over the
county border into Cumbria. The return is via Arnside Knott
with splendid views of the Lakes and along the coast. Good
paths all the way and little chance of slutch.

🔘 Park your car on the slip road to the beach, or when it is busy in
the car park in the village. Follow the path along the grassy salt
marsh, close to the land, for just over quarter of a mile until the
cliff bends inland to the Cove.

ℹ️ *This salt marsh has long been grazed by both sheep and cattle, otherwise
there would be an abundance of flora to be found here. However in
recent years much of this marsh has disappeared due to the River Kent
finding a new channel out into Morecambe Bay. This apparently occurs
every 60 or 70 years. Until the end of the nineties the channel was
more out to sea towards the Grange shore but now it flows near to the
coast at Park Point (which you will as later in the walk). The result
is the salt marsh has largely been eroded revealing the pebbles and rocks
beneath leaving only the short stretch at the beginning of the walk.*

🔘 Continue along the pebbly beach and scramble round the rocks
till you can go no further and then strike up right to a gate and
onto the road. Turn left and follow the road, taking great care
since quite a lot of cars use this stretch, and follow this for about

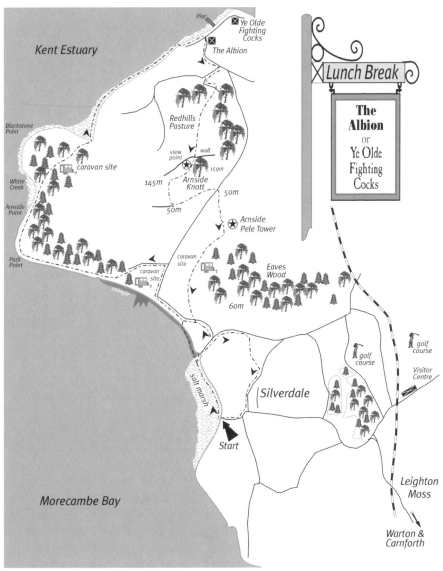

Kent Estuary

Pier

Ye Olde Fighting Cocks

The Albion

Blackstone Point

caravan site

White Creek

Amside Point

Redhills Pasture

view point   wall

145m

Arnside Knott

159m

50m

50m

Arnside Pele Tower

Park Point

caravan site

shingle

caravan site

Eaves Wood

6om

salt marsh

Silverdale

golf course

golf course

Visitor Centre

Start

Morecambe Bay

Leighton Moss

Warton & Carnforth

Lunch Break

The Albion

or

Ye Olde Fighting Cocks

Silverdale to Arnside

N

Looking north up the River Kent towards the Arnside viaduct, with the rocky footpath clearly to be seen.

half a mile. Just past Priory croft turn left down the lane and go through the caravan park at Far Arnside where, once in the site, you take the right fork at the signpost in the direction of the footpath.

Do take care as you walk along this path. It goes very near to the edge of a steep cliff, and it is easy to be distracted by the splendid views across Morecambe Bay.

After about 1,000 yards you arrive at Arnside Point where you bear right through White Creek caravan park to New Barns. Turn right along the lane and as you go over the bridge turn left and walk along the beach.

The going can be quite tricky as you walk the last mile into Arnside, especially if it is a very high tide. However, there is always lots to see especially if you are a student of seaside flora: pink thrift, sea and buckshorn plantain, common gromwell, scurvey grass and black bryony can all be found in their time. For bird lovers there are always ringed plover and redshank and over in the trees on your right you may hear wrens as they angrily announce ownership of their own piece of territory. Occasionally the combination of a neap tide, a stiff westerly wind and heavy rainfall swelling the River Kent means this path is totally under-water, in which case follow the road into Arnside.

123

(🚶) The shore path eventually emerges onto the promenade and after 200 yards you are in the centre of Arnside. (4.25 miles; 1 hr 45 mins) There are two pubs here: *The Albion Hotel* or *Ye Olde Fighting Cocks*, which is just about 100 yards further along in the direction of Sandside.

(🚶) Leave whichever pub you have chosen for lunch and turn left up Silverdale road towards The Knott and at the top turn right along Redhills road and then take High Knotts road up to the left and at the top turn sharp left along a row of expensive-looking detached houses. After about 150 yards turn right up a path through trees and eventually over a stile into a field, known as Redhills Pasture and which, during the early years of the twentieth century, was used as a 9-hole golf course.

(ℹ) *There are conflicting ideas behind the name 'Redhills'. Some say it is because iron ore was once mined here and the hollows are the remains of excavation. The other theory is that salt was extracted here and the remaining humps are the red spoil left behind from that exercise.*

(🚶) Head up the field for the highest point, there is a vague path you may notice delineated by darker green grass, and when you come to the wall go through the gate, turn right and follow the track gently up towards the top of Arnside Knott (500 ft). Go through a gate in the wall and bear right up to the lookout where you'll have a good view of the Lakeland Fells and the Kent Estuary on a good day. The top of the Knott is marked by a trig point in the trees behind you about 100 yards away.

(ℹ) *Should you be here in July or August you may see one of Arnside Knott's special butterflies, the Scotch Argus. This is a brown butterfly with two sets of four spots on the outer edge of its wings. This butterfly is only found in two places in England, the Arnside/Silverdale Area of Outstanding Natural Beauty (AONB) being one of them. It particularly enjoys the scabious flowers and the blue-moor grass on which it lays its eggs. Another rare butterfly to be found in the area is the High Brown Fritillary which enjoys a habitat of limestone and violets which are also to be found here. This light-brown butterfly has black markings on the upper side of its wings and the rear underside wing has white markings on it. Bird spotters may wish to look out for green and greater spotted woodpeckers but you'll know they don't fly out to greet you! Blue Moor grass is only found in England and Arnside is the western*

*National Trust
volunteers clearing
trees to encourage the
growth of the unique
'blue moor' grass to
be found at Arnside.*

*extremity of the slim band of this rare grass which stretches from near
Malham in the Yorkshire Dales across through the limestone country
to Morecambe Bay. It is so called because when it flowers late in
February it is as though a delicate blue haze hovers over the grass.
Tne National Trust takes particular care in preserving the grass by
removing trees which have only grown during the past 50 years since
the Knott stopped being grazed by cattle; a process which the NT is
gradually reintroducing.*

From the seat bear left and down and at the first junction of the
track turn left, by a bench, down through the trees and to a gate.
Through this follow the path down and at the junction of paths
turn left on to the bridle way and down hill to the main road at
Hare Parrock.

*As you go down this path up on your left are The Shilla Slopes. These
are very steep limestone screes created by glaciers during the last Ice
Age.*

When you go onto the road do take care, there are cars about!
Cross over and down the lane to the farm and Arnside Tower. At
the farm go up, not to the left, and take the path which goes past
the ruined fourteenth-century pele tower on your left and then up
and over the stile into the woods of Holgate's Caravan Park.

*Pele towers (pronounced 'peel') were fortified buildings, mainly built in
the fourteenth century to protect farmers and their livestock from plunder-
ing Scots. This example is one of a number in the area. They are to
found all over the north of England but there are not many south of
the Lune.*

125

(人) Carry straight on and up and then at the road through the site turn right and make for the central buildings. Before you get to them bear left and across a short field and over a stile onto the road. Turn left but don't turn right down the lane to Red Rake which you came up earlier but continue towards Silverdale. Just past the bowling club take the unmade road to your right and past houses on your left and into the centre of the village. At the crossroads turn right and back down to the slip road where you parked your car earlier. (3.75 miles; 1 hr 30 mins)

Walk 22

Warton to Silverdale

Outdoor Leisure Map 7:   *The English Lakes SE Area*
Distance: 9 miles.   Walking time: 3 hrs 45 mins
Start at the car park on Crag Road, grid ref. SD 497724
Lunch at *The Silverdale Hotel,* 01524 701206

T HIS WALK starts with a stiff ascent of 120 metres (460 ft)
up to the beacon on Warton Crag before dropping down
to sea level again and then another ascent of 50 metres
(165 ft) up Heald Brow. Then the route meanders through
woodland and fields to Silverdale for lunch before returning
along the coast, with slight undulations, and returning
across the edge of Leighton Moss before the return over
Warton Crag.

❶ *Crag Road is up by the side of the George Washington pub on Main
Street in Warton, it was previously known as The Black Bull. The
pub name was changed in about 1998 because the family from which
George Washington was descended lived in Warton. The family built
the tower of St Oswald's church and each 4th July 'Stars and Stripes'
are flown from the tower in honour of the village's illustrious progeny.*

🚶 Leave the car park by the footpath at the top end of it next to
the rock face and this leads directly upwards to the top of Warton
Crag, an Area of Outstanding Natural Beauty.

❶ *It is also partially a Nature Reserve and a Site of Special Scientific
Interest too. It is indeed a very special area and as well as being
partially managed by Lancaster City Council, the RSPB and Lancashire
Wildlife Trust have responsibilities. As you gradually climb what is
known as 'The Lower Terrace' you will begin to have good views over
Morecambe Bay and you may also notice tree pipits, blackcaps and
whitethroats, which are common on the crag, and don't forget to look
out for butterflies in the summer; in particular the High Brown Fritillary
for which the crag is one of the most important sites in the country.
They thrive on limestone and violets and both are to be found here.*

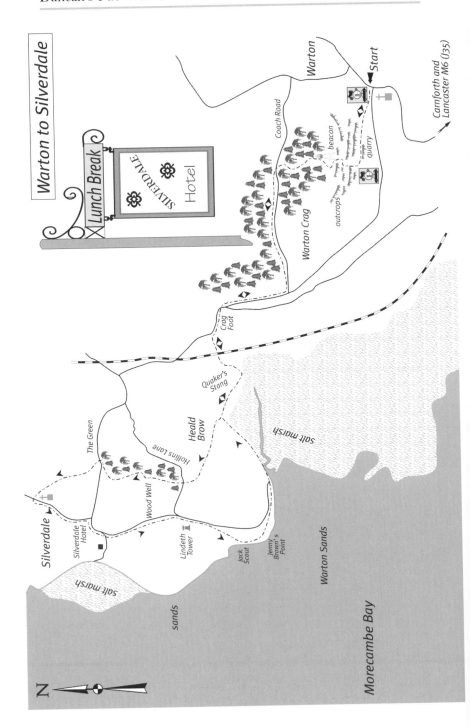

Warton to Silverdale

Lunch Break

SILVERDALE Hotel

Warton

Start

Carnforth and
Lancaster M6 (J35)

Coach Road

beacon

quarry

Warton Crag

outcrops

Crag
Foot

Quaker's
Stang

Salt marsh

Heald
Brow

The Green

Hollins Lane

Wood Well

Silverdale

Silverdale Hotel

Lindeth
Tower

Jack
Scout

Jenny
Brown's
Point

Warton Sands

Salt marsh

sands

Morecambe Bay

N

*Warton Crag, the
beacon.*

After the initial scramble up a rather steep path scattered with limestone, which can be rather slippery in or just after wet weather, you go through a wicket gate where you turn right uphill and then immediately left by the big stone. Carry on upwards and keep to the right hand track where there is one. You soon come to a stile with the old quarry car park down below on your left, so go over the stile and after about 30 yards turn sharply right up hill and ascend to the summit. This involves a bit of scrambling here and there but if you keep going up you will arrive at the right place. Having scrambled up and over two craggy outcrops you come to a wall with a gap stile in it. The path levels off for a few yards but up on your right there is another outcrop and a stile at the bottom of it. Go over and scramble up the rocks which is quite easy since it is a bit like climbing stairs. Soon after passing through some bushes you come to the top where there is a wonderful lookout place.

You can look north and west and on a good clear day see up and down the coast as well as towards King William's hill behind Silverdale and further away Arnside Knott. Behind the Knott you will spot a wide range of the Lakeland Fells. Right down below you are the Keer Marshes and Quaker's Stang, the flat grassy plain, and Jenny Brown's point. Over on your left, to the south, is Morecambe and Heysham. Also here is a beacon erected in 1988. The first one was put there in the thirteenth century and one of the occasions when it was lit would have been to warn of the approach of the Spanish Armada in 1588. The new beacon commemorates this event. Long prior to that a Celtic fort had been built but remains of this are not obvious. There are in fact three concentric rings of ramparts covering an area of about 15 acres (6 hectares) but because of the scrub and trees, not to mention the grasses and paths and other factors, the ramparts are almost undicernible.

(🚶) Take the path straight ahead from the Beacon and at the junction take the right hand path pointing to 'Coach road & Warton'. At a Y junction take the left hand path indicated by a white arrow on a stake. Soon you come to a wall and next to the gate is a gap stile out onto to the Coach road which is also known as Occupation Road, an ancient track which goes over the top of the crag north to south. Turn left and follow the lane all the way down to Crag Foot and the road. Turn right downhill and at the bottom carry on following the road towards Silverdale. Soon you will see a finger post on the other side of the road just before you enter Silverdale, as indicated by the City of Lancaster sign. Follow the path alongside the sluice and under the railway bridge. Then first right over the bridge to follow the 'Lancashire Coastal Way' along the top of an embankment which surrounds Quaker Stang. The embankment is there to keep the sea out.

(ℹ️) *A 'stang' is a 'stake or post marking a boundary' which suggests this was once land owned by a quaker; though I've often wondered if it wasn't a place where Quakers were martyred on a stake. After all, this area was a stronghold of Quakers in the seventeenth century and more than one of them was killed by over-enthusiastic supporters of the established church. As you walk along the embankment you may see some interesting birdlife on either side of you but more than likely on the seaward side where you will see many waders at all times of the year.*

(🚶) At the end of the embankment you climb over a stile and go through a gate on your right and then take the left hand path uphill to Heald Brow. The path has marker stones so you can't get lost. The path goes through a wall and straight on. You will see a gate through the trees but don't head for this; go up a bit to your right and then left to a gap stile in the wall next to which is a galvanised water trough. The path follows the wall on your left through a field and as you come to the lower end you go over a stile and then head for a gate. Turn right and walk down a path between a wall and a hedge. Through a gate at the bottom you then see another gate out onto the road, Hollins Lane, where you turn right and across the road is a sign post to 'Woodwell', so go through the gap and down through the trees. The path goes alongside a fence and on your right is a limestone cliff and some interesting flora, in which no doubt you may also detect some interesting fauna if you have the patience! At the end of this short path you go through a gate and to your right is a well below an outcrop of limestone.

ℹ *Until the first few years of the last century this was one of the sources of fresh water to the inhabitants of the area. The water percolates through the limestone and drips into the man built trough below. It then leads off to another series of troughs: a big oblong holding trough and a narrow one with two sections which are thought to be where the local women came to do their washing. No one seems certain but one of my companions remarked that it was very similar in arrangement to something he had seen in the south of France and which was still being used for washing clothes. My guess is that it was used for washing fleeces. As well as the water dripping into the well there is also water oozing out of the face of the limestone crag. Since the crag is shady and never receives direct sunlight algae forms on the limestone and the lime water gradually hardens to form 'tufa' which is smooth and much treasured by water gardeners who are known to sneak into this area and chisel it away during the hours of darkness. This is strictly illegal with heavy fines; so if you see someone looking suspiciously like a tufa thief it is up to you to do something about it. The main bird speciality of these woods is the elusive hawfinch but to spot one of these you will have to remain still and quiet. Although 'resident' they are best seen in winter and early spring.*

(⚐) The path now leads upwards as indicated by the finger post 'The Green via cliff path' and there is another scramble up the limestone outcrop. Once again it is quite easy since the 'steps' all seem to be in the right place. Do take care though when it is wet. At the

The 'Coach Road' or 'Occupation Road' as it is sometimes known.

top turn left and soon take a right turn and walk over some 'pavement' which again can be slippery when wet. Soon this brings you to a wider path. On your left is a stile into a small pasture where you then go to the right and up a slope beside a big protected tree. Bear left at the top and then you go over another stile where the path goes through the trees, with a small pasture down on your left. You approach a house and beside the door the path goes alongside the wall to the house and then after going over another stile you are on a good track which leads you out onto the road. Cross over and turn right and then take the path indicated to 'The Church', soon you leave the tarmac and go to the left to follow the path to 'Emesgate Lane' going past a big house on your right before going through another gap stile next to a gate into a field. The path follows the wall which is on your left and at the bottom there is a five barred gate to the left of which is a wicket gate next to the wall. Go through this and then out onto Emesgate Lane. Turn left and walk into the centre of Silverdale. At the junction with Shore Road turn right and follow the pavement until you come to *The Silverdale Hotel* where you will get a good bar meal or snack. (4.6 miles; 2 hrs)

🚶 Turn left out of the pub and at the junction bear right up Lindeth

Lindeth Tower, often referred to as 'Gibraltar Tower', where Elizabeth Gaskell often stayed.

Road. Follow this road for about 800 yards and at the junction take the right fork. Lindeth Tower will soon be on your right.

ⓘ *This tower, also known as 'Gibraltar Tower' since it stands next to Gibraltar farm and is on a rock standing high and prominent as seen from the seashore, looks ancient but is in fact a folly built in 1842 by Sir Peter Fleetwood Hesketh as a holiday hideaway. The three-storey building has one room on each floor. Mrs Elizabeth Gaskell, the Cheshire author of* Wives and Daughters *and many other books, stayed here often. Even though she described it as 'a queer crampy house', she loved its glorious views over Morecambe Bay.*

ⓧ Soon, on your right, is the entrance to the National Trust's Jack Scout area so go through the gate and follow the path towards the sea. It bears left through bushes and soon emerges on the cliff top with the sea down below on your right. Follow the path until you eventually emerge out onto the road again. Soon you will come to Jenny Brown's Point where the lane ends and you go down on your right to the salt marsh.

🛈 *Jenny Brown was the inhabitant of a house here in the eighteenth century but sadly little is known about her, or her family, other than the fact that she kept pigs!*

🚶 Follow the path along the shore, passing by the lime kiln chimney, until you come to the embankment on your right along which you walked earlier. Follow the path along the top of the embankment, then under the railway bridge and along the track to the road. Turn right and then, just as the road turns to the right, take the left hand fork up Windy Scout Brow.

🛈 *The old, square stone chimney with bricks at the top quarter is all that remains of a nineteenth-century pumping station built to pump water from Leighton Moss out into the sea. It ceased operating at the end of the First World War.*

🚶 From here you simply retrace your steps back over Warton Crag and to your car. (4.4 miles; 1 hr 45 mins)

Walk 23

Williamson Park, Lancaster, to Caton

Outdoor Leisure Map 41: Forest of Bowland & Ribblesdale
Distance: 9.8 miles. Walking time: 3 hrs 40 mins
Start at Williamson Park car park, grid ref. SD 488610
Lunch at *The Ship*, 01524 770265

MOST OF THIS WALK follows good firm paths, some of which can have large puddles after wet weather. It provides good views north towards the Lakes and is one of the few with an urban start, through the fascinating park which is worth a visit of its own. Other than a gentle climb up from the Lune on the return journey the going is reasonable horizontal.

(※) Leave the car park and go to the left hand end as you enter the car park. Walk along a short path to the entrance of the park and then up the drive to the Ashton Memorial where you turn right up the main path to the butterfly house.

(ⓘ) *The memorial was built by Lord Ashton, a millionaire who made his fortune making linoleum, as a memorial to his wife. Inspired, it is said, by the Taj Mahal, it was completed in 1909. It is used frequently for cultural events and on the second floor is the Williamson Gallery where frequent art exhibitions are displayed. The Butterfly House has a fine collection of butterflies and moths which fly freely and behind is a 'mini-beast' collection.*

(※) Pass in front of the café and shop and this path takes you down to Quernmore Road where you turn right to find Stone Row Head about 300 yards further down on your left. This road leads to Lancaster Farms Prison and just before you get to the entrance of it there is a car park on waste land to your right and a bridleway, known as Moor Lane. Go down this lane and the prison fence will be on your left. Soon the lane approaches the M6, where you turn right and cross over the motorway by the bridge and continue walking northwards along Grimeshaw Lane, which is

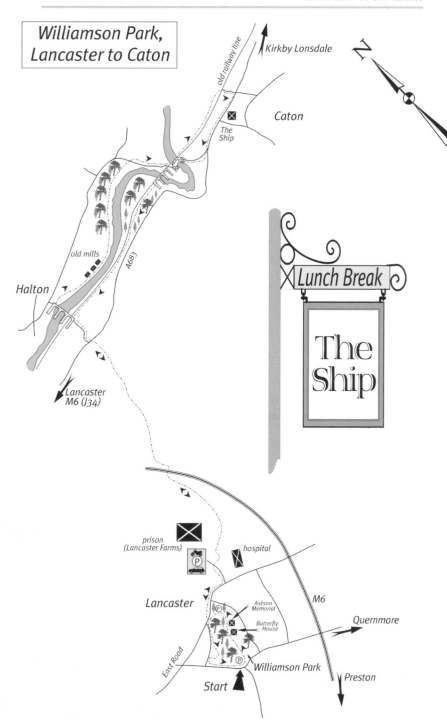

Williamson Park, Lancaster to Caton

old railway line

↑ Kirkby Lonsdale

Caton

The Ship

old mills

A683

Halton

↙ Lancaster M6 (J4)

Lunch Break

The Ship

prison (Lancaster Farms)

hospital

Lancaster

M6

Ashton Memorial

Butterfly House

Quernmore

East Road

Williamson Park

Preston

Start

another farm track and a bridleway.

ⓘ *You get some wonderful views north to the Lakeland Fells, west over Morecambe Bay and east towards Ingleborough and the Dales as you walk along this lane.*

⬤ After about a mile the lane comes out onto the A683 from Lancaster to Kirkby Lonsdale. Taking great care, since the traffic comes fast here, cross over and go down the narrow Denny Beck lane opposite to the left of the house. This is also a busy lane since it is a quick route into Halton, over the narrow bridge which you will cross in about five minutes. So keep alert and well to the side of the roads and in single file if there are a few of you. Whilst crossing the bridge you will probably stop and admire the Lune.

ⓘ *There has been a bridge here since 1869 and a newer, wider bridge was opened in 1913 though it is still quite narrow and only suitable for small vehicles. Until the trains stopped running on the Lancaster*

'Bulk Bridge' over the River Lune at Halton.

*The old oak and
fishstones at Caton.*

to *Wennington line there was a toll for crossing over and foot passengers
paid 1d. (pre-decimal penny) which in modern terms is less than half
a penny. You may even have time for a game of 'Pooh Sticks' if you
remember to pick up some suitable sticks before you set off across to the
other bank.*

Once over the bridge take the first right, Mill Lane, and walk past
the various workshops until it starts to rise up and overhead is a
power line. Here go right between the buildings towards the river
which you should be able to see from the track.

*As you walked along the lane past the workshops you may wish to
reflect that in times gone by this was a very busy place where a number
of textile mills were situated to take advantage of the fast-flowing Lune.
One of the mills, Low Mill, produced in turn: silk, cotton, coconut
matting and oilcloth goods. As you walk along the river you will
understand why this was such a popular spot to build a mill, especially
if it is in full flood. During the times when the river was not flowing*

with its full force a millpond was used, situated above the mills up the slope, and was fed by a race which left the river roughly where the weir is now.

Turn left and follow the path alongside the river until you come to the weir. Here you go up the steps and then follow the path through the woods. This path gradually rises up and emerges out onto a road and this too can be dangerous if you don't take care. Cross over then follow the pathway which runs parallel to the road behind the wall. This leads you onto the car park at Crook o' Lune, so turn into it and then right onto the other section where you will also find a convenient WC. You might also find 'Woody's' van there from where you can purchase a drink and something to eat if you're so inclined. Proper mugs and newspapers too! Cross the car park in the direction of the old railway line, just to the left of the exit out onto the road, and go down the steps. At the

The old railway station on the Lune Valley Cycleway, near to Halton Bridge.

bottom turn left, over the bridge and follow the path for about half a mile, then turn right into Caton at the Old Railway Station and by the Catholic Chapel. In Caton you can stop for lunch at the splendid pub, *The Ship*, which is on the main road about 100 yards on your right and across the road. (5 miles; 1 hr 50 mins)

❶ *Caton is another ancient village, and mentioned in the Domesday Book as 'Catun': from the Norse 'farmstead or village of a man called Kati'. Near to The Ship Inn stands an old oak tree which seemingly just about survives but has looked weary for many years and is cleverly propped up. Fish stones circle the tree where monks reputedly sold their catches of Lune salmon. Most stories say the monks were Premonstratensians from Cockerham Abbey but it is more likely they were from the Priory of the same order near to Hornby.*

⏑ Whichever pub you eat in turn left and follow the road back towards Lancaster then turn right at the junction, towards Halton and Crook o' Lune. Just before the bridge take the path on your right and this soon puts you back on the old railway line.

❶ *The railway line was opened in 1850 running from Lancaster to Wennington where it joined the Skipton to Carnforth line. It was known as the 'Little' North Western Railway so it wouldn't be confused with the London North Western. One of the Directors of the company was Edmund Sharp who later bought Halton Hall, now all but demolished. He was responsible for the purchase of rolling stock which on delivery was found to be unsuitable in a variety of ways; the prime one being that it was too wide for the line which at its opening wasn't the standard gauge. Passenger services stopped in 1965, at the same time that tolls stopped being collected on the bridge.*

⏑ So turn left and over the bridge again and carry on all the way to the old Railway Station at Denny Beck Lane. Here you turn left and follow the lane back to the A683 and across it, still taking care to watch out for fast moving vehicles. Then you simply retrace your steps up Grimeshaw Lane and Moor Lane to Quernmore road. Turn right and then left into the park and back to your car. (4.8 miles; 1 hr 50 mins)

Walk 24

Yealand Conyers to Silverdale

Outdoor Leisure Map 7:   The English Lakes SE area
Distance: 8 miles.   Walk time: 3 hrs 25 mins
Start at the centre of Yealand Conyers, grid ref. SD 504746
Lunch at *The Royal*, 01524 701266

JUST ONE OF MANY ENJOYABLE WALKS to be had in this delightful corner of Lancashire, an 'Area of Outstanding Natural Beauty'. The ascents are few and gentle and the views are varied. The walk takes in woodlands and secret pools, open meadows, a wildfowl centre and takes you past an tree almost older than history. Very good under foot but after long periods of rain, particularly in winter, the path through Leighton Moss may not be passable due to the pools overflowing and the low level of the path.

Parking places are few and far between here but you should find a space down one of the side roads but do make sure you're not blocking anyone in.

Set off by going back onto the main road through the village and up the steps to the pasture on the west side of the road, up above the wall. Bear left and head up the field in the direction of a marker pole you will see. Carrying on across the drive to Yealand Manor go up to the gate in the top left hand corner of the field and through this turn right. Follow this path through the trees with the Manor down below on your right. The path goes down to a gate and through into the field the right of way running through the middle of it. At the far end of the field there is a gate, which you don't pass through, but to the left you will see a set of steps going up through the limestone rocks which is the way to go. Through the rocks follow the path over two stiles and then down into Deepdale wood. Further down the path approaches an outcrop of rock reaching up and above you. The path bends to the right here and goes steeply down to Deepdale pool. Pass by the pool and go up to the junction where you turn to the left. Soon you

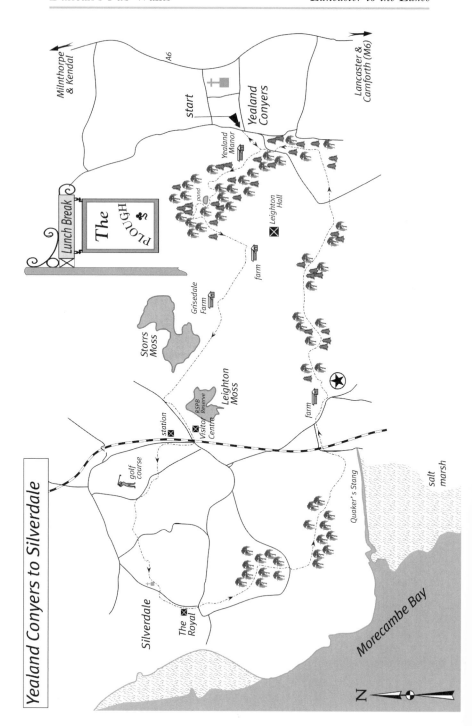

Yealand Conyers to Silverdale

The 'small-leaved lime'. Local tradition has it that it is 5000 years old.

emerge from the woods and as you walk through two fields you will see Leighton Hall over to your left and ahead of you.

ⓘ *A house was first built on the site now occupied by the hall in 1246 but this was destroyed by Government troops in 1715, following the capture of its owner at the time, Alfred Hodgson, a supporter of the Jacobites. It was rebuilt in 1763 and the present neo-Gothic facade was added in 1825 by the Gillows who, like all but one of its owners, were Roman Catholic. The present owners are related to the Gillows who made fine furniture in Lancaster and on display are some fine examples of their work. Tours of the house are usually during the summer months and there is also a fine display of birds of prey.*

ⓧ At the track to the hall turn right and just past the farm on your right bear right to follow the path through the middle of Leighton Moss RSPB Reserve with the reed beds and pools on both sides of you.

ⓘ *The reserve occupies 321 acres, an ornithological paradise which is one of the most important in the country for water fowl and where almost a third of those visiting breed and rear their young. As you walk along the track it is well worth while stopping at one of the hides for a few* *minutes to spend time watching the birds. Inside the hides displays point out the varieties you are likely to spot.*

(✹) This long straight track leads you out onto a road where you turn left and then take to the courtesy path you will see on your left. This ends near to the RSPB visitor centre so walk on the road, which is often busy just here, over the railway bridge and to the junction. Turn right, with the golf clubhouse on your left, and past the old railway station. About 25 yards further on cross over to the left to take a path across the golf course. It is well marked with yellow arrows but do look out for little white balls flying through the air. You do have right of way but 'courtesy never faileth' and it is easier for you to stop than one of the balls! The path rises up to a wall at the other side of the course and a gate leads out onto The Row, where you turn right and follow the road gently uphill for about 250 yards until it starts to go down and round a rather nasty right hand bend, so keep to the left here and not the usual right hand side facing the oncoming traffic. At the safety railings go through the gate in the wall and follow the path across two fields. In the third one turn left and follow the wall to a gate onto a road. Cross over and bear right to another gate on your left and follow the path, with the wall on your left,

The old pumping house chimney at Crag Foot.

heading in the direction of the church spire in the distance. The path cuts through the wall to the left and continues along the wall which is now on your right. Through a gate, with houses on your left, you then come to a junction where you turn left and keep to the right where you will see bungalows ahead. Continue ahead and onto the main road through Silverdale. Turn left and soon you will be at The Royal where you can have your lunch. (4 miles; 1 hr 40 mins)

(🏃) Leaving the pub turn right and walk down to the junction where you turn left and cross over the road to take the footpath to Woodwell. This path goes past the backs of many houses and as it emerges into the woods take the path to the left and then the next left.

(❶) *One of the interesting points about the Silverdale/Arnside area is the rich variety of flora and fauna, many species of which are almost unique to the area or are extremely rare. One of these is a small-leaved lime which you will pass and which is on your right hand side. It would be quite easy to pass by this and not even notice it but on closer examination you will see a long tangle of trunk sitting atop a small limestone outcrop which stretches for about twenty feet. Springing up from this tangle of wood are a number of stems. What is remarkable is that this multi-stemmed tree is clearly ancient, although local tradition insists it is a rather amazing 5,000 years old!*

(🏃) The path meanders on through the trees until soon you are near to a small reservoir or lodge.

(❶) *This water was part of the early system of public water supply to the village and is fed by a spring which erupts from the limestone outcrop some twenty yards away.*

(🏃) Go to the right of this and then follow the path alongside a field on your right and bushes and shrubs on your left through which is a limestone outcrop before going up a short sharp incline through the trees out onto the road. Cross over and bear slightly right and then through the gate on your left and then through the left hand gate in front of you. At the top of this short path go through the gate on your left and follow the wall on your right. At the next wall go over the stile and bear diagonally right to the bushes and small trees and follow the path left and down through the bushes and trees on Heald Brow. At the bottom Leighton Moss will be in front of you and here you turn right and then left over the stile to follow the embankment round what is known as Quaker's Stang. The saltmarsh down on your right extends a good mile before it gives way to the sands of Morecambe Bay. The path takes you to a bridge over The Pool and then under the railway before leading you out onto the road. Here turn right and then cross over just before you reach Crag Foot and the chimney.

ⓘ *This chimney is all that remains of a pumping station that worked night and day during the latter days of the nineteenth century and up until the end of the First World War in order to drain the surrounding area.*

ⓧ Follow the track to Moss House farm turning right just before you reach it and then almost immediately left to follow the narrow path through the trees. Soon this emerges onto a track so follow this through the gate ahead of you and then bear right across the field. The track then leads you up to a 'Private' sign where you bear left and through a gate to follow the path, with the woods on your left, through a long, narrow field which rises gradually up. Go over the stile and carry on before turning sharp right to go up the field towards the outcrop with trees on it. Past this you will find a well trodden path up through more trees to a stile through a wall. Carry on straight ahead through a field and soon onto a track which eventually brings you out onto a road. Cross over and into the field and carry straight on up this and eventually gently down through a few bushes and trees. Soon you will spot ahead a small white gate in the wall on your right but you don't go through the gate but bear sharp left and follow the path through the rather rough pasture. A gate at the top lets you out onto a road where you turn right and then after about 50 yards you take a gap stile on your left, just before the bend. Once again keep on the left hand side of the road. Through the stile you bear to the right towards the little gate, which you passed through earlier, before going down through the pasture and then down the steps onto the road and back to your car. (4 miles; 1 hr 45 mins)

Walk 25

Yealand Storrs to Arnside

Outdoor Leisure Map 7:   *The English Lakes SE area*
Distance: 9.5 miles.   Walking time: 3 hrs 55mins
Start at junction of Storrs lane with Thrang Brow Lane,
grid ref. SD 494762
Lunch at *The Albion* (01524 761226)
or *Ye Olde Fighting Cocks* (01524 761203)

A WALK in the Silverdale/Arnside area always has a rich variety of interest in it and this is no exception. It takes you through mature woodland, up to see the Silverdale 'Pepperpot', across fields and up Arnside Knot with an ascent of about 40 metres (130 ft) before you arrive in Arnside for lunch. The return walk is without any real ascent and takes you back to the car via the wetlands around Hawes Water.

There's just enough room to park about three cars off the road as you turn right to go up Thrang Lane towards Arnside, so park here next to the remains of the wall and go back to the junction. There, on your right, you will see a gate leading into the wooded area known as Yealand Hall Allotment.

This is not the sort of allotment found in urban areas where householders without gardens can grow their own vegetables and flowers, but an historical allotment of land going back hundreds of years to a time when the land was allotted possibly by the king or an earl to the owner of Yealand Hall.

Walk through the wood following the path which goes straight ahead. It emerges out of the wood into an area of sporadic trees and bushes and follows a wall on your left. After about 200 yards you look out for a gap stile, next to a gate, into the field over on your left. Go over it and walk diagonally to the right across the field towards a gap in the wall and a signpost. Don't go through the gap but turn sharply left and walk along the boundary which will be on your right. Soon you enter some trees and you follow

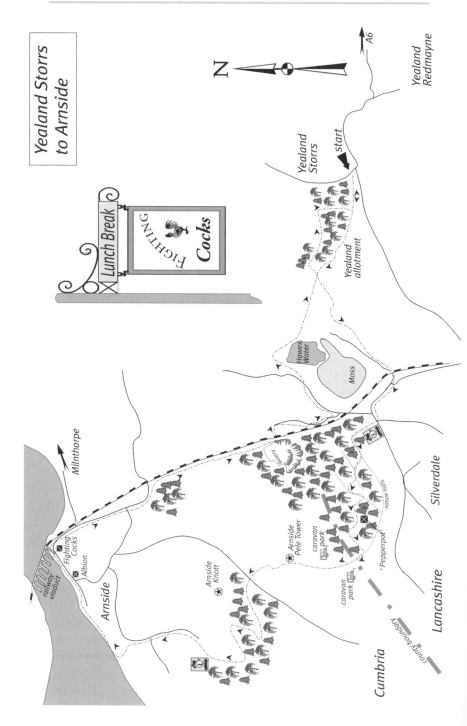

*Silverdale 'Pepper
Pot commemorating
Queen Victoria's
Golden Jubilee in
1887*

the path down which soon turns left and gradually down through
the trees before it emerges over a stile into a field. Keep following
the path going gradually down and more or less follow the
boundary on your right, over which are a number of sheds and
other buildings, some of which are dwellings. This path brings
you to a stile next to a gate and onto a lane where you turn left
and then, just as you pass over the railway line, you come to a
junction. Turn right here and although it is only a narrow road
it is usually quite busy, so keep alert, to the right and walk in
single file. At the next junction carry straight on towards Silverdale but turn right up the entry on your right to a small car park
where you will see a National Trust sign. Go through the gate
and straight ahead to turn left at the junction. You are now in
Eaves Wood, a NT reserve so make sure you keep to the paths.

ⓘ *This mature wood is situated on a long limestone ridge contains a rich variety of trees and shrubs, both deciduous and evergreen, and is worth a visit just to wander around its pathways and drink in the unique, almost 'magical' atmosphere. Species spotters will be overwhelmed by the sheer number of birds, insects, animals, flowers, trees, shrubs and fungi to be found here. Surely a lifetime would not be long enough to count them all! Especially keep an eye open for the elusive hawfinch which feed in the canopy. If you don't see it you may well hear its short 'ptik' or its longer high pitched 'sip'. You will also see small leaved lime trees and a local species of whitebeam, only to be found on the limestone on the edge of Morecambe Bay.*

(🚶) After about 200 yards a path goes to the right and up so take this and after a while there is a junction with another path coming from your right. Carry on and then take the next turn on your right which also leads uphill. Soon you come to a clearing with a large multi-stemmed beech tree in the centre. Continue straight on and the path rises gently upwards, all the while bearing in a westerly direction. Another path joins from the right and you carry on bearing to the left and soon you arrive at another junction. Turn sharp right here and you then walk on the level for a while before rising up again and passing through a wall. Carry straight

Arnside Tower with the shilla slopes on the south side of Arnside Knot in the background.

The remains of Arnside Tower seen from the west.

on with a limestone outcrop on your right resembling a concrete wall. Soon there is another junction and here you go upwards through the trees on your left. In a minute or two you arrive on a limestone plateau and there in front of you is what is known colloquially as the 'Pepper Pot'.

ⓘ *You will realise very quickly that the 'Pepper Pot' is just a simple cairn built to celebrate Queen Victoria's Golden Jubilee in 1887 but you won't need much of an imagination to work out how it gained its name. If you read the tablet set into the cairn you will note that it doesn't actually refer to the Golden Jubilee and it is obvious that at the time the patriotic locals who erected it never expected Queen Victoria to last another ten years and celebrate her Diamond Jubilee. From here you get a good view of Silverdale village to the south and over to the west the southern end of Morecambe Bay.*

🧍 Leaving the 'Pepper Pot' turn your back on it and take the path bearing to the left. You soon drop down a through limestone crag to a hollow and then up again where you bear right at the next junction and soon come to a wall. Turn left and drop down over another few layers of limestone, which can be slippery when wet like all limestone, and down to another few layers. Carry on down, through a gap and out of Eaves Wood. Not much further down you come to another path where you turn right and through a gap in the wall and from Lancashire into Cumbria. On your left, through the trees you will see a caravan site. Carry on this path with the caravans close to you on your left and eventually you

arrive on the main drive of the caravan site. There will be a
children's playground on your left. Bear slightly to the right before
going left up a road with a 'No road' sign, red circle and white
bar. Go up this for 20 yards and as it slightly bends right, opposite
the first tree on your right, go left across the grass and down into
the bushes to find a path which should lead you past the ruins of
Arnside Tower. Across over on the southern slopes of Arnside
Knot you will clearly see the 'Shilla Slopes' of loose limestone and
just over the tree line the top of the Tower. Go down through
the trees and soon you come to a ladder stile over a wall; go over
and past the tower.

ⓘ *This is a pele tower built in the fourteenth century at a time when
marauding Scots came down over the border to seek anything worth
while. During the time they were in the area the family and some of
the stock of the farm would barricade themselves into the fort until
danger had passed. The 'Shilla Slopes' are very steep limestone screes
which were left behind by the receding glaciers at the end of the last
Ice Age.*

(☤) The path goes down to the farm and once through it you follow
the farm track up to the road below Arnside Knott. Just across
the road is a gate leading up the side of the Knott and you follow
this upwards, with the shilla slopes you saw earlier up on your
right, through a gate and straight on. When the path levels off
somewhat you come to a junction with another path on your right,
turn up the path which leads up to a gate. Go through and then
on uphill on a rather rough path made of limestone chippings. At
the top there is a bench, turn left here. Then after about 50 yards
take the right fork in the path and uphill through the trees until
you come to a wall and a gate or gap and a 'lookout' just ahead.

ⓘ *The wall was originally built about 1821 but gradually fell into disrepair
following the Second World War. The National Trust decided to
rebuild it and a number of volunteers gathered and stacked stones for
one man to do the craft work. His name is Eric Shorrock, a 'National
Trust' volunteer who, at the time of writing, is in his mid-seventies
and still going strong and completing up to four yards of wall during
a good week. Eric is proof that you're never too old to learn a new
skill and he is convinced that his work keeps him alert and fit. The
'lookout' has descriptive panels and you will have a good view of*

Arnside and the Kent estuary down below you, together with a panoramic view of the south east Lake District; a view of breathtaking wonder at all seasons of the year, particularly when the distant fells aren't obscured by clouds or banks of rain!

🧍 Bear to your left and take the zig-zag path down which is quite steep. Eventually you come to a wall with a gap stile in it. Don't go through but turn right and follow the path down with the wall on your left until you come to the car park. Keep going straight ahead and soon you will be on the access road to the Knott going downhill into Arnside. As you leave the National Trust land you emerge onto Knott lane and this runs into Redhills Road. Turn right and eventually you come to a footpath sign on your left. Follow this down to the shore and turn right and soon you will be on the promenade. After about 150 yards you will come to *The Albion* or about 100 yards further on *Ye Olde Fighting Cocks* where you can have some lunch. (5.3 miles; 2 hrs 15 mins) Both pubs are good for a bar snack and a drink so take your choice.

🧍 Leaving the pub, whichever one you've been in, turn right and walk along Station Road but don't turn left to go under the railway bridge, carry straight on along Black Dyke Road. After about half a mile the road bends left and crosses the railway track but you take the footpath at the right hand side of the road which carries straight on and eventually, after dodging through some rather tatty buildings, follows the railway on your left hand side. So far

National Trust volunteer, Eric Shorrock, completing another stretch of wall over Arnside Knot.

this part of the walk has been pretty uninteresting, and you will have to walk across about 800 yards of rather flat meadow before you enter some woods. Still carry straight on and then you come to a quarry. The entrance is over the railway line but if you look straight ahead you will spot a footpath sign just by the quarry gate ahead of you. This takes you round the back of the quarry offices and soon another signpost indicates the way. Go up through the trees and bear left and keep left. After about 200 yards there is a fork so keep right but don't go uphill. Eventually the path goes down to your left and emerges at the entrance to a garden centre. Turn right and follow the drive to the road. Here turn left and at the next fork turn right. Then, just past Challan Hall the big house on your right with apartments to let, look out for a footpath which goes off diagonally on your right into land controlled by English Nature.

This takes you round Hawes Water, which you may have glimpsed earlier in the day, and is on your right.

ⓘ *Hawes Water is just another of the many interesting nature sites in the Silverdale/Arnside area with an abundance of species far too many to detail and again a place where a whole day could be spent just spotting a few of the delights to be found here.*

🚶 The path turns sharply round to the right and then brings you very close to the water. Here you take a footpath on your left and eventually to a wicket gate. The path then goes through two fields, going diagonally right across them, before you go through a gate stile and find yourself in a place you were earlier on in the day. However don't retrace your steps but turn sharp left and walk towards the corner of the field and through a gap stile, then turn right to follow the track through the trees. After a left hand turn in the track you approach a gate; don't go through this but take a turn to the right and then through the bushes and bracken you go over a stile into an opening of rough ground and you are in Yealand Hall Allotment again. The path goes straight on and veers left and up. Then after about 250 yards turn right into a narrow neck in the meadow and over a stile. This leads you straight down and to a junction with another path and you are on the path on which you started out. Turn left and soon you will be back at your car. (4.2 miles; 1 hr 45 mins)